MW01283746

Blood,

The Currency Of The Spirit World

By

Jacqueline Trought

Blood, The Currency Of The Spirit World
by Jacqueline Trought

Printed in the United States of America

ISBN 9781626977235

Unless otherwise indicated, Bible quotations are taken from the King James Verison of the Bible.

www.xulonpress.com

Dedicated to my husband, Winston, whose insistence caused me to reach beyond and find the truth and wealth of the presence of God. Also to Mya, my granddaughter, who keeps inspiring my vision.

Table of Contents

CHAPTER 1

Life is in the Blood

I have set before you life and death, choose life, that both you and your children may live. —Deuteronomy 30:19

In the beginning, God created the heavens and the earth, the light and the darkness, the firmament and the animals. "And the Lord God formed man of the dust of the ground, and breathed into his nostrils the breath of life; and man became a living soul." (Genesis 2:7) The breath of God entered the lungs, traveled to the heart and eventually entered into the blood. Blood circulating throughout the body carried the breath of God—or rather, the breath of life. Blood then, is the carrier of life.

Anatomically, bones contain marrow, and the marrow churns out stem cells that form the tissue we call blood. Blood is the only tissue that has constant contact with every cell of the body. Apart from carrying the life of God—or as we so appropriately term it, oxygen—blood feeds the body with nutrients and assists in the process of extracting wastes. Yet another important function is maintaining a balanced environment so that the body may be comfortable to continue its normal functions. The red color of blood is attributed to little red cells suspended in the liquid; white cells are also found in the suspension, and they act in the capacity of defense. The liquid portion of blood has a clear, watery look if all these cells—red cells, white cells, and other particles—are removed. Often, blood cells are extracted and tested to identify blood type—sort of a label that marks the blood—while other blood tests can determine the state of health of the body.

The blastocyst of the developing fetus (the beginning stages of a baby in the womb) consists of dividing cells allocated to internal organs and external body structures. From these cells, just around the fifth week after conception, the heart, spinal cord and brain will develop. Shortly after, the major blood vessels form, and the heart begins to pump blood with its first red blood cells. Where does that breath come from in this developing embryo? Does God breathe again each time conception occurs? No. The sperm and the egg are alive. They carry life; they carry the breath of God. This life is ready for its existence on earth—ready to carry out the will of God, its creator.

The enemy has no legal right to the breath in man; man's breath belongs to God. Therefore, it is also true that the enemy has no legal ownership to man. Man belongs to God; man was created and made alive for God and His divine purpose. However, Satan has constantly lusted and connived for the glories of God—the lives of humans are now his chief priority. Life can then be redefined as serving the Creator, or on the other hand, being beguiled by him whose sole existence is to steal the life of God from mankind. If he has no legal right to the lives of humans, then every life that Satan adds to his coffers has been stolen. The master of deception negotiates his way into the heart of man through the promise to fulfill the needs and insatiable desires of the flesh; in the process, he works to bring devastation to the body or waste precious life through the spilling of blood, resulting in death.

CHAPTER 2

Smooth Deception

> I gave my heart to seek and search out wisdom concerning all things done under heaven: this sore travail has God given to the sons of man to be exercised therewith. —Ecclesiastes 1:13

> Hell from beneath is moved for you to meet you at your coming: it stirs up the dead for you, even all the chief ones of the earth; it has raised up from their thrones all the kings of the nations. All they shall speak and say unto you, "Are you also become weak as we? Are you become like unto us?" Your pomp is brought down to the grave, and the noise of your viols: the worm is spread under you, and the worms cover you. How art thou fallen from heaven, O Lucifer, son of the morning! How art thou cut down to the ground, which didst weaken the Nations! For you have said in your heart, I will ascend into heaven, I will exalt my throne above the stars of God: I will sit also upon the mount of the congregation, in the sides of the north: I will ascend above the heights of the clouds; I will be like the Most High. Yet you shall be brought down to hell, to the sides of the pit. They that see you shall narrowly look upon you, and consider you, saying, "Is this the man that made the earth to tremble, that did shake kingdoms; that made the world as a wilderness, and destroyed the cities thereof; that opened not the house of his prisoners?" (Isaiah 14:9–18).

The story above is told of an angel named Lucifer. The Son of the Morning was beautiful to look at, and was God's right hand.

Lucifer, now referred to as Satan, coveted the throne of God; he along with one third of the angels in heaven, committed anarchy to displace God.

The plot failed, and Satan was kicked out of heaven with the rebellious angels. However, he has not given up on the scheme to disrupt the plan of God. The turf has changed, and so has his strategy, but the plot continues. Since his fall from grace, Lucifer's scheme has been to violate the relationship between God and His children by deceiving the children into rejecting their Father God.

As a result of the fall, another kingdom was born, ruled by Lucifer and the fallen angels. Of course, the subjects of both kingdoms—the kingdom of Jehovah God and the kingdom of Lucifer—are not humans, but angels. They are referred to as supernatural beings, which means they are empowered beyond human abilities. The habitation of these beings is also beyond human comprehension, except that humans are given a glimpse into this spiritual realm from time to time.

The two spiritual kingdoms are distinctly set apart by right and wrong, good and evil. Hence, they are referred to as the kingdom of light and the kingdom of darkness, respectively.

The kingdom of God operates on the premise of truth with unaltered foundational standards. The children of God's kingdom have bargained, reasoned and deliberately written amendments to the laws of God, but all have failed in the light of the purity and stability of the Word of God, which is firmly unchangeable. Psalm 12:6 tells us that the Words of the Lord are pure words; like silver is tried in a furnace of earth, so the Word is purified seven times.

The kingdom of darkness began its existence in treason. Satan exalted himself to take God's throne, and along with the angels that joined in the botched overthrow, he was cast out of God's domain into the lake of everlasting fire. The goal of the satanic kingdom is to accomplish evil at any cost. With deception at its helm, the regulations are tailored specifically to bring death to the soul of man.

When God created Adam in the Garden of Eden, He gave Adam the unique gift of authority over all that was created. The Lord God specifically referred to the gift as *dominion*—subdue and rule the earth. The clause 'dominion' included the wholesomeness of enjoyment and complete delight in the beauty of all that was created.

God came down in the cool of the day to fellowship with Adam and Eve. He gave them liberty to enjoy the garden in which they lived, except one tree from which they were told not to eat. One day, when God was not around, Satan visited Eve and had an interesting conversation with her. In this conversation, he accomplished a most sinister plot. The Devil caused the woman to look beyond her capacity and conceive of the notion that her environment could be enhanced by simply bending an unimportant rule. As soon as he was satisfied that she was sufficiently duped, he dropped out of site. The Devil tricked Eve into disobeying God. (Genesis 3:19)

Eve trusted the words she heard from God's enemy. To demonstrate her belief, she followed through on the words she heard. Eve perhaps had no desire to taste of the fruit of the forbidden tree. God, whom she and Adam loved, did not want her eating of the tree, and that was enough. However, another opinion caused her to think twice. I wonder how long it was after the conversation with Satan that Eve became convinced to do that which she had never done before?

The Devil's words were, "You will become like gods." (Genesis 3:5) What an exciting proposition. Is there any higher achievement? All that Eve possessed paled in the light of this offer. "I will offer you the ability to be like god; just do as I say." This may have been the sweetest lie to land on the ear of mankind. Amazingly, the same line is used today to beguile many. But look again—has anyone achieved the status, or even come close to being god?

Interestingly, an unholy exchange took place. There were fine prints—or rather, in this case, an undertone to the Devil's words. If Eve obeyed his words, she would become his servant. As a servant, all she possessed would be turned over to him for ownership. What did Eve own? Land—lots of it. This is an understatement; sorry! Eve owned all of it. Let's not forget the intrinsic value to the land—*dominion*. There is a difference between owning and possessing. Adam and Eve possessed the land, the earth.

Another point to consider is the knowledge of God. Adam and Eve possessed infinite knowledge that was stolen in a moment of trickery. Holy, undefiled humans who fellowshipped with God daily, and were filled with the knowledge of God (talk about holy communion), became void of God's glory in a moment and instead were filled with fear.

It is safe to say, then, that fear is a product of sin—of disobedience to truth—and at the root of fear is shame. From that point forward, Adam and Eve conducted their lives in shame. How could they return to the state of purity, the safety of the perfect love of God? Notably, after sin was accomplished, it created the rift that separated Adam and Eve from all they had enjoyed and possessed, and they did not know how to re-inherit or re-establish the bond needed to save them from this dreadful state.

Before the beguilement, Adam and Eve communicated daily with God on subjects of creation and the holiness of God's being—the questions we crave answers for. Who is God? Where does He come from? My granddaughter asked, "When is God's birthday?" She wanted to give Him birthday presents. This and more generated the serenity and sweetness that oozed from both parties as they enjoyed the delicacy and purity of worship. Those moments ruptured the infinity of time as man became lost in indescribable pleasure, serenading Love as He was designed to be reverenced, and Love reciprocating with the infilling of His Spirit. So the two became one, melded in thought and mind, allowing the exchange of fellowship to flow homogeneously without words, yet with potent understanding, intense joy and an unlimited exchange of ideas, like swift currents of light; they were loaded.

It is hard to imagine that the master of trickery and deception won the rights to Adam and Eve's minds, actions and future—and he took it all. Not just from Adam and Eve, but from all their descendants. Psalm 51:5 says, "Surely, I was sinful at birth, sinful from the time my mother conceived me" (NIV). He took the knowledge, the land, the dominion and the fellowship, and left man deprived and in a stupor.

The theory, "you will become like God" was long forgotten in a tangled mess of abandonment. See, Satan did not reveal the whole truth; he never does. His bill of goods is sold on false promises, and when he does not deliver, there is no reclaim of lost value or clobbering the monster over the head for robbing us blind. We are left entirely on our own to sort out a godless existence and pending doom.

It may be a good time to ask what was God's response to all this. Well, God sent His Son, Jesus, to earth to become the bearer (or the Christ) for the sins of Adam and his descendants through a sacrificial death by crucifixion. And in like manner, Satan offered Jesus a deal. Luke 4:5–7 captures it in this way: "Jesus, son of God, bow down and worship me, reverence me, obey me, and I will give You all the kingdoms of this world and the glory of them, for they have been delivered to me and I give it to whomever I wish." If Jesus accepted this offer, He would not have had to die for the sins of mankind.

The exchange would have been the reclaim of that which Lucifer stole from Adam and Eve—dominion, possession, *et cetera.* However, the rest of the deceptive clause would read, "Jesus never became Christ (Savior of the world), because He entered into an unholy alliance with Satan when He bowed and worshiped the enemy of God. He got the world and its glory, but He never reclaimed the lost souls of humanity. As a result, He was not able to go back to His Father, God. Of course He was ashamed, but the most damning result was that God lost complete fellowship with His children, and they are all subject to grotesque evils in their lives on earth, and after death, they enter the flames of eternal hell." But Jesus was not swayed by the cunning lies of Satan. Jesus knew Satan could not deliver on any promise. He is just a liar; in fact, he is the father of lies.

Should we belabor the point that the plot continues? Everyone who flees the camp of Satan to serve the living God will come face-to-face with the decision to accept the subtle offer of selling his or her soul, to accept the ease and pleasure of that which the eye can see and the heart passionately desires but has not yet attained. The offer to sell is never for the salvation of man's soul. (Of course, the enemy will lie, but any fool will know he does not have salvation.) The offer is only for the limitations of fleshy indulgence, and the limits are multiplied to gain trust, but the Devil cannot deliver. The bottom line is that Satan is still hunting prey. He has never stopped, and the snake charm of his subtle, lying offers need eyes of the spirit to decipher.

It does bring up the question, with the intensity of fellowship experienced between Adam, Eve, and God, and their subsequent failure, who then can qualify for an undefiled relationship with this holy God? I am glad you asked. Let's sigh with relief for the pure and precious blood of Jesus Christ, Son of the living God.

CHAPTER 3

Religion through Various Eyes

Consider and hear me, O Lord my God: enlighten mine eyes, lest I sleep the sleep of death. —Psalm 13:3

Man has ran the gamut on religion. If it is out there, someone is going to find it. If it does not exist and someone envisions it, bet your bottom dollar it will be created. Why? Man was created to worship.

Some of us have accepted the concept that if there is a God out there somewhere, He must be bigger and greater than our minds would allow us to perceive. Therefore, our faith rests in the revelation He has handed to us. The mystery that surrounds His omniscience, omnipresence, and omnipotence will suffice, because anything less reduces Him to our limitations. Our search is diligent and unstoppable. Our reverence is deep. Our explanation is beyond words, so we humbly express ourselves in steadfast faith.

Still, others have placed their faith in God through humans or objects. This faith seeks its connection not directly but rather through a sincere trust in the ability of someone or something else to communicate with the God in whom he or she trusts but has not connected. Then, there are religions that have conferred sanctity upon gods they see with physical eyes. This makes absolute sense to the physical man, whose intellect is trained to maneuver and conquer his world. Therefore, if one cannot see it, taste it, touch it, smell it, or feel it, the limited mind says it cannot exist.

Other religious forms trust in self to analyze the maze of life and connect to inner peace or the lack of it. Again, this belief carries the idea that if the concept cannot be explained in its fullness—if it leaves gaps of unanswered questions or unsuitable definitions—then it lacks the qualifications to satisfy complete submission and worship. The worshiper here creates a god rooted in self. Uniquely, the inadequacies are so endless that this religion leads to the search for more, and eventually skews rights and wrongs, truths and lies. Grasping for solutions, it creates ambiguous answers to define the unexplainable, and with the eventual control of those in its grasp, it cries out, "This is power, and I am god."

There is more. Some have formulated rituals and rites that confer upon them qualifications to increase and rise above the status quo and achieve the unthinkable. In these notions lie the belief that one has tapped into the realms of higher powers that rule and activate that which tantalizes the senses and bestows a sort of greatness above peers. This then becomes the milestone, the marker that ushers him or her beyond; greatness becomes godliness.

Please forgive my ignorance, because it is hard to fathom each man's notion of God; for even those who congregate to honor the lord of a common faith differ in understanding and knowledge of the god they serve. But we must explore this last facet of another type of religion. There are those who worship Lucifer as god. Fascinating information exists on the doctrine and the rituals performed by these followers, but most intriguing were the depth of trust and the passion expressed by them.

At its foundation, all religion obligates its followers to some form of worship where the god being served requires due diligence in return for the conferral of that which its subjects seek. The exchange between god and man, and the requirements of the exchange, take matters to levels unimaginable. A newspaper of the Congolese reported a father who was required to cohabit with his two-year-old infant and bring the blood to the witchdoctor. In exchange, he and his family would no longer be poor. Okay, this is bizarre. Where did this father place his heart when he went to commit this blood sacrifice? What kind of poverty could reduce a father to that level of cruelty?

Of course, there are ritualistic practices requiring the burning of bodies—animal or human; practices that require gruesome piercings and markings on the body; practices that require babies to be offered by fire to the gods in exchange for what is considered a great life here on earth; and we cannot forget the ultimate sacrifice of one's own life to a god or in the name of religion in exchange for a better life hereafter.

And you shall not let any of your children pass through the fire to Molech, neither shall you profane the Name of thy God: I am the LORD. (Leviticus 18:2)

And they caused their sons and their daughters to pass through the fire, and used divination and enchantments, and sold themselves to do evil in the sight of the LORD, to provoke Him to anger. (2 Kings 17:17)

And he made his son pass through the fire, and observed times, and used enchantments, and dealt with familiar spirits and wizards: he wrought much wickedness in the sight of the LORD, to provoke Him to anger. (2 Kings 21:6)

My point is that some religions and their requirements are strange. Okay, I have once again understated a major point. The measures humans have gone to attain the dream of life as we know it has left the planet in mourning. Beyond the devastation wreaked are the lies, cover-ups, hatred, wars and division that have been generated; yet the promise was to attain greater and better things. Is this a revelatory moment to ask, "If my achievement was indeed better, then why is my soul in such agony and shame?"

Perhaps for those of us who have not been rendered calloused by the deeds and promises of an unfulfilling religion, the soul may still wait for truth. Perhaps somewhere out there exists a God who can rectify and restore, who can truly make crooked places straight, who can restore the breach, who can make all things work together for my good if I choose to love Him, who has a way that is right and the end is not destruction. Perhaps that which I need is truly beyond what my mind can perceive.

Is it possible to believe in simple trust that the Almighty God must be beyond my explanation? Could the reality be that a childlike faith bears the solution to true peace and prosperity? But how can I truly know who God is? Was it not my belief that led me to the place I am? How can I trust my knowledge to yield righteousness?

The secrets of life are hidden to those who are proud in spirit, but a broken and contrite heart, God will not refuse.

CHAPTER 4

A Time of Meditation

> When wisdom enters into your heart, and knowledge is pleasant unto your soul; discretion will preserve you, understanding will keep you. —Proverbs 2:10

Now the birth of Jesus Christ was like this: When as His mother Mary was engaged to Joseph, before they came together, she was found with child of the Holy Ghost. Then Joseph her husband, being a just man, and not willing to make her a public example, was minded to put her away privately. But while he thought on these things, behold, the angel of the Lord appeared unto him in a dream, saying, Joseph, thou son of David, fear not to take unto you Mary your wife: for that which is conceived in her is of the Holy Ghost. And she shall bring forth a son, and you shall call His name JESUS: for He shall save His people from their sins. Now all this was done, that it might be fulfilled which was spoken of the Lord by the prophet, saying, Behold, a virgin shall be with child, and shall bring forth a son, and they shall call His name Emmanuel, which being interpreted is, God with us. Then Joseph being raised from sleep did as the angel of the Lord had told him, and took unto him his wife. (Matthew 1:18–24)

And in the sixth month the angel Gabriel was sent from God unto a city of Galilee, named Nazareth, to a virgin engaged to a man whose name was Joseph, of the house of David; and the virgin's name was Mary. And the angel came in unto her, and said, Hail, you that are highly favored, the Lord is with you: blessed are you among women. And when she saw him, she was troubled at his saying, and cast in her mind what manner of salutation this should be. And the angel said unto her, Fear not, Mary: for you have found favor with God. And, behold, you shall conceive in your womb, and bring forth a son, and shall call His name Jesus. He shall be great, and shall be called the Son of the Highest: and the Lord God shall give unto Him the throne of His father David: And He shall reign over the house of Jacob for ever; and of His kingdom there shall be no end. Then said Mary unto the angel, "How shall this be, seeing I know not a man?" And the angel answered and said unto her, "The Holy Ghost shall come upon thee, and the power of the Highest shall overshadow thee: therefore also that holy thing which will be born of you shall be called the Son of God. And, behold, your cousin Elisabeth, she has also conceived a son in her old age: and this is the sixth month with her, who was called barren. For with God nothing shall be impossible." And Mary said, "Behold the handmaid of the Lord; be it unto me according to your word." And the angel departed from her. (Luke 1:26–38)

For unto us a child is born, unto us a son is given: and the government shall be upon His shoulder: and His name shall be called Wonderful, Counselor, The Mighty God, The everlasting Father, The Prince of Peace. Of the increase of His government and peace there shall be no end, upon the throne of David, and upon His kingdom, to order it, and to establish it with judgment and with justice from henceforth even forever. The zeal of the LORD of hosts will perform this. (Isaiah 9:6–7)

For God so loved the world that He gave His only begotten Son, that whosoever believes in Him will not perish but have eternal life. For God sent not His Son into the world to condemn the world; but that the world through Him might be saved. (John 3:16–17)

Come unto Me, all you that labor and are heavy laden, and I will give you rest. Take My yoke upon you, and learn of Me; for I am meek and lowly in heart: and you shall find rest unto your souls. For My yoke is easy, and My burden is light. (Matthew 11:28–30)

Repent you therefore, and be converted, that your sins may be blotted out, when the times of refreshing shall come from the presence of the Lord. And He shall send Jesus Christ, which before was preached unto you: Whom the heaven must receive until the times of restitution of all things, which God hath spoken by the mouth of all His holy prophets since the world began. For Moses truly said unto the fathers, "A prophet shall the Lord Your God raise up unto you of your brethren, like unto me; Him shall you hear in all things whatsoever He shall say unto you." (Acts 3:19–22)

But this is a people robbed and spoiled; they are all of them snared in holes, and they are hid in prison houses: they are for a prey, and none delivers; for a spoil, and none says, "Restore." Who among you will give ear to this? Who will hearken and hear for the time to come? (Isaiah 42:22–23)

Surely He hath borne our grief, and carried our sorrows: yet we did esteem Him stricken, smitten of God, and afflicted. But He was wounded for our transgressions, He was bruised for our iniquities: the chastisement of our peace was upon Him; and with His stripes we are healed. All we like sheep have gone astray; we have turned everyone to his own way; and the LORD hath laid on Him the iniquity of us all. (Isaiah 53:4–6)

He was oppressed, and He was afflicted, yet He opened not His mouth: He is brought as a lamb to the slaughter, and as a sheep before her shearers is dumb, so He opened not His mouth. He was taken from prison and from judgment: and who shall declare His generation? For He was cut off out of the land of the living: for the transgression of my people was He stricken. And He made His grave with the wicked, and with the rich in His death; because He had done no violence, neither was any deceit in His mouth. Yet it pleased the Lord to bruise Him; He hath put Him to grief: when you shall make His soul an offering for sin, He shall see His seed, He shall prolong His days, and the pleasure of the Lord shall prosper in His hand. He shall see of the travail of His soul, and shall be satisfied: by His knowledge shall my righteous servant justify many; for He shall bear their iniquities. Therefore will I divide Him a portion with the great, and He shall divide the spoil with the strong; because He hath poured out His soul unto death: and He was numbered with the transgressors; and He bare the sin of many, and made intercession for the transgressors. (Isaiah 53:7–12)

Who His own self bare our sins in His own body on the tree, that we, being dead to sins, should live unto righteousness: by whose stripes you were healed. For you were as sheep going astray; but are now returned unto the Shepherd and Bishop of your souls. (1 Peter 2:24–25)

Then said Jesus unto his disciples, If any man will come after Me, let him deny himself, and take up his cross, and follow Me. (Matthew 16:24)

For I am not ashamed of the gospel of Christ: for it is the power of God unto salvation to everyone that believes; to the Jew first, and also to the Greek. For therein is the righteousness of God revealed from faith to faith: as it is written, The just shall live by faith. (Romans 1:16–17)

But blessed are your eyes, for they see: and your ears, for they hear. (Matthew 13:16)

For this purpose the Son of God was manifested, that He might destroy the works of the devil. (1 John 3:8)

This I recall to my mind, therefore have I hope. It is of the LORD's mercies that we are not consumed, because His compassions fail not. They are new every morning: great is Thy faithfulness. The Lord is my portion, says my soul; therefore will I hope in Him. The Lord is good unto them that wait for Him, to the soul that seeks Him. It is good that a man should both hope and quietly wait for the salvation of the Lord. (Lamentations 3:21–26)

The wilderness and the solitary place shall be glad; and the desert shall rejoice, and blossom as the rose. It shall blossom abundantly, and rejoice even with joy and singing: the glory of Lebanon shall be given unto it, the excellence of Carmel and Sharon, they shall see the glory of the Lord, and the excellence of our God. Strengthen you the weak hands, and confirm the feeble knees. Say to them that are of a fearful heart, "Be strong, fear not: behold, your God will come with vengeance, even God with a recompense; He will come and save you." (Isaiah 35:1–4)

Wisdom is the principal thing; therefore get wisdom: and with all thy getting get understanding. Exalt her, and she shall promote thee: she shall bring you to honor, when you do embrace her. She shall give to your head an ornament of grace: a crown of glory shall she deliver to you. (Proverbs 4:7–9)

Can a woman forget her sucking child, that she should not have compassion on the son of her womb? Yes, they may forget, yet will I not forget you. Behold, I have graven thee upon the palms of My hands; your walls are continually before me. (Isaiah 49:15–16)

Have you not known? Have you not heard, that the Everlasting God, the Lord, the Creator of the ends of the earth, faints not, neither is weary? There is no searching of His understanding. He gives power to the faint; and to them that have no might He increases strength. Even the youths shall faint and be weary, and the young men shall utterly fall: But they that wait upon the Lord shall renew their strength; they shall mount up with wings as eagles; they shall run, and not be weary; and they shall walk, and not faint. (Isaiah 40:28–31)

Heal me, O Lord, and I will be healed; save me, and I will be saved: for You are my praise. (Jeremiah 17:14)

And again I say unto you, "It is easier for a camel to go through the eye of a needle, than for a rich man to enter into the kingdom of God." When his disciples heard it, they were exceedingly amazed, saying, "Who then can be saved?" But Jesus beheld them, and said unto them, "With men this is impossible; but with God all things are possible." (Matthew 19:24–26)

I am the door: by Me if any man enter in, he shall be saved, and will go in and out, and find pasture. The thief comes not, but for to steal, and to kill, and to destroy: I am come that they might have life, and that they might have it more abundantly. I am the good Shepherd: the good Shepherd gives His life for the sheep. (John 10:9–11)

I am the good Shepherd, and know My sheep, and am known of Mine. As the Father knows Me, even so know I the Father: and I lay down My life for the sheep. (John 10:14–15)

My sheep hear My voice, and I know them, and they follow Me: And I give unto them eternal life; and they shall never perish, neither shall any man pluck them out of My hand. My Father, which gave them to Me, is greater than all; and no man is able to pluck them out of My Father's hand. (John 10:27–29)

I love the Lord, because He has heard my voice and my supplications. Because He has inclined His ear unto me, therefore will I call upon Him as long as I live. The sorrows of death compassed me, and the pains of hell got hold upon me: I found trouble and sorrow. Then called I upon the Name of the Lord; "O Lord, I beseech thee, deliver my soul." Gracious is the Lord, and righteous; yes, our God is merciful. The Lord preserves the simple: I was brought low, and He helped me. Return unto your rest, O my soul; for the Lord has dealt bountifully with you. For You have delivered my soul from death, my eyes from tears, and my feet from falling. (Psalm 116:1–8)

Be it known unto you all, and to all the people of Israel, that by the Name of Jesus Christ of Nazareth, whom you crucified, whom God raised from the dead, even by Him does this man stand here before you whole. This is the stone which the builders rejected, which is become the head of the corner. Neither is there salvation in any other: for there is none other name under heaven given among men, whereby we must be saved. (Acts 4:10–12)

He brought them out, and said, "Sirs, what must I do to be saved?" And they said, "Believe on the Lord Jesus Christ, and you shall be saved, and your house." And they spoke unto him the Word of the Lord, and to all that were in his house. And he took them the same hour of the night, and washed their stripes; and was baptized, he and all his, straightway. (Acts 16:30–33)

For when we were yet without strength, in due time Christ died for the ungodly. For scarcely for a righteous man will one die: yet peradventure for a good man some would even dare to die. But God commends His love toward us, in that, while we were yet sinners, Christ died for us. Much more then, being now justified by His blood, we shall be saved from wrath through Him. For if when we were enemies, we were reconciled to God by the death of His Son, much more, being reconciled, we shall be saved by His life. And not only so, but we also joy in God through our Lord Jesus Christ, by whom we have now received the atonement. Wherefore, as by one man sin entered into the world, and death by sin; and so death passed upon all men, for that all have sinned: (For until the law sin was in the world: but sin is not imputed when there is no law. Nevertheless death reigned from Adam to Moses, even over them that had not sinned after the similitude of Adam's transgression, who is the figure of Him that was to come. (Romans 5:6–14)

Therefore, just as sin entered the world through one man, and death through sin, and in this way death came to all people, because all sinned—To be sure, sin was in the world before the law was given, but sin is not charged against anyone's account where there is no law. Nevertheless, death reigned from the time of Adam to the time of

Moses, even over those who did not sin by breaking a command, as did Adam, who is a pattern of the One to come. But the gift is not like the trespass. For if the many died by the trespass of the one man, how much more did God's grace and the gift that came by the grace of the One man, Jesus Christ, overflow to the many! Nor can the gift of God be compared with the result of one man's sin: The judgment followed one sin and brought condemnation, but the gift followed many trespasses and brought justification. For if, by the trespass of the one man, death reigned through that one man, how much more will those who receive God's abundant provision of grace and of the gift of righteousness reign in life through the One man, Jesus Christ! Consequently, just as one trespass resulted in condemnation for all people, so also one righteous act resulted in justification and life for all people. For just as through the disobedience of the one man the many were made sinners, so also through the obedience of the One man the many will be made righteous. The law was brought in so that the trespass might increase. But where sin increased, grace increased all the more, so that, just as sin reigned in death, so also grace might reign through righteousness to bring eternal life through Jesus Christ our Lord. (Romans 5:12–20, NIV)

Your Word have I hid in mine heart, that I might not sin against You. (Psalm 119:11)

But what says it? The Word is near you, even in your mouth, and in your heart: that is, the Word of faith, which we preach; that if you will confess with your mouth the Lord Jesus, and will believe in your heart that God has raised Him from the dead, you will be saved. For with the heart man believes unto righteousness; and with the mouth confession is made unto salvation. For the scripture says, Whosoever believes on Him shall not be ashamed. For there is no difference between the Jew and the Greek: for the same Lord over all is rich unto all that call upon

Him. For whosoever shall call upon the Name of the Lord shall be saved. (Romans 10:8–13)

Then Jonah prayed unto the Lord his God out of the fish's belly, and said, "I cried by reason of mine affliction unto the Lord, and He heard me; out of the belly of hell cried I, and You heard my voice. For You had cast me into the deep, in the midst of the seas; and the floods compassed me about: all Your billows and Your waves passed over me." Then I said, "I am cast out of Your sight; yet I will look again toward Your holy temple. The waters compassed me about, even to the soul: the depth closed me round about, the weeds were wrapped about my head. I went down to the bottoms of the mountains; the earth with her bars was about me forever: yet have You brought up my life from corruption, O Lord My God. When my soul fainted within me I remembered the Lord: and my prayer came in unto You, into Your holy temple. They that observe lying vanities forsake their own mercy. But I will sacrifice unto You with the voice of thanksgiving; I will pay that which I have vowed. Salvation is of the Lord." And the Lord spoke unto the fish, and it vomited out Jonah upon the dry land. (Jonah 2)

Order my steps in Your Word: and let not any iniquity have dominion over me. (Psalm 119:133)

Being confident of this very thing, that He which has begun a good work in you will perform it until the day of Jesus Christ. (Philippians 1:6)

Grace be to you, and peace, from God our Father, and from the Lord Jesus Christ. Blessed be the God and Father of our Lord Jesus Christ, who has blessed us with all spiritual blessings in heavenly places in Christ: According as He has chosen us in Him before the foundation of the world, that we should be holy and without blame before Him in love: Having predestinated us unto the adoption of children by Jesus Christ to Himself, according to the good pleasure of His will, to the praise of the glory of His grace, wherein He has made us accepted in the beloved. In whom we have redemption through His blood, the forgiveness of sins, according to the riches of His grace; Wherein He has abounded toward us in all wisdom and prudence; Having made known unto us the mystery of His will, according to His good pleasure which He hath purposed in himself: That in the dispensation of the fullness of times He might gather together in one all things in Christ, both which are in heaven, and which are on earth; even in Him: In whom also we have obtained an inheritance, being predestinated according to the purpose of Him who works all things after the counsel of His own will: That we should be to the praise of His glory, who first trusted in Christ. In whom you also trusted, after that you heard the Word of truth, the gospel of your salvation: in whom also after that you believed, you were sealed with that Holy Spirit of Promise. (Ephesians 1:2–13)

And the God of peace shall bruise Satan under your feet shortly. The grace of our Lord Jesus Christ be with you. Amen. (Romans 16:20)

As for Me, this is My covenant with them, says the LORD; My spirit that is upon you, and My Words which I have put in your mouth, shall not depart out of your mouth, nor out of the mouth of your seed, nor out of the mouth of your seed's seed, says the LORD, from henceforth and forever. (Isaiah 59:21)

Forever, O LORD, Your Word is settled in heaven. (Psalm 119:89)

CHAPTER 5

Blood for Redemption

Why is blood so important in the spirit world, and how did it earn its distinction as spiritual currency?

At the fall of Adam and Eve, God instituted a spiritual principle—the death of one by the shedding of blood for the redemption of another—when He provided covering for them from the skin of animals. The shedding of blood was given for the remission, or rather, the pardon of sins. Blood was used to render man symbolically purified from sin. Later, Noah appeased God's heart with a sweet smelling savor of blood offerings when the episode of the ark was ended (Genesis 8). In the Levitical writings, as God established the law for His own Nation, He commanded them to bring burnt offerings, fellowship offerings, sin offerings and guilt offerings, all from the shedding of blood. Various Scriptures state that the shedding of blood, burnt by fire, is an aroma pleasing to God.

The children of Israel, before they became a nation, were in the bondage of slavery in the land of Egypt for over four hundred years, and God decided to end the atrocity. He said to His servant, Moses, "I have heard the cry of My children, and I have come down to help them." (Exodus 3:7) Well, did God lift a finger? No, instead He gave specific instructions. All that God commanded proved His might and miraculous power, but when the time was fully come for the deliverance to take place, His instructions were that the people shed blood.

Does blood activate and deactivate bondages in the spirit, moving beyond the mere destruction of physical chains? Yes—the children of Israel are living proof. Their bondage manifested physically in brutal labor when they built the Egyptian empire. Logically, there must have been plots of escape, plans to overthrow the government, rebellion and boycott. Moses himself offered his services by killing an Egyptian whom he thought wronged an Israelite, but nothing budged. In fact, life only got harder. However, when God announced the day of deliverance, He required of the hands of the wounded blood sacrifice with specific instructions.

Let's reason this out. An entire nation was in bondage, suffering cruelty at the hands of merciless taskmasters, crying out for 430 years to the God they served and receiving no answers, but crying nonetheless; and then God answers their desperation by giving instructions on the shedding of blood. The answer was so potent, it relieved more than half a million men (not counting children) of the mental, emotional and physical bondage that encapsulated generations and engraved itself on their culture. It transformed slaves into soldiers, servants into leaders, and instruction-takers into nation-builders.

Sin brings death to the soul of man. In fact, sin is the thief of a great life. Romans 6:23 tells us that the wages of sin is death, but the gift of God is eternal life (through the shed blood) of Christ Jesus, our Lord. Shed blood was the satisfactory price, offered and accepted, that released the spiritual bondage and physical chains of Israel.

To whom was the blood offered? Who held the spiritual chain of bondage? Who owns me? Who benefits if I die? Why does death have such an impact on humans? What is the significance of my blood?

When Jesus Christ was on the cross, He said, "It is finished; man's redemption is paid." In Hebrews, the writer tells us that after His death and resurrection, Jesus went into heaven itself and presented the Father God with the pure sacrifice of His shed blood as a lasting atonement for all who choose to accept God's plan of salvation. This tells us that shed blood is offered to the master who requests the sacrifice. Each time blood is shed to satisfy spiritual rituals, it becomes payment for the task at hand. Therefore, the payment is the sacrifice—the life offered, or the life taken. The payment is then presented to God or the Devil, and the blood that is spilled covers the person or answers the request made at the offering of the sacrifice.

How does the system of redemption work? Technically, sinners are servants of the Devil. He owns sinners. To be made righteous or be in right standing with God would then necessitate a purchase of the sinner from the owner. In our given system of trade, purchases necessitate even exchanges; owners walk away from the bargaining table with substances of equal value. Is the shed blood of Jesus Christ offered to the Devil as atonement for the sin of mankind? No, the holy blood of Jesus Christ, shed for the pardon of sins, is not given to the Devil as an exchange for a life.

Without question, the Devil cannot accept the purity of the holy blood of Christ, or he would be made pure; neither is there any trade or exchange of goods for a price. Instead, when anyone, the whomsoever, did whatever (except blasphemy against the Holy Ghost), upon repentance, and consciously by will, asks for the pardon that comes with the shed blood of Jesus Christ, the blood of Christ that was handed to the Father by the Son is applied to the repentant heart. This blood purifies the heart and mind, releases the soul from the grip of the bondage of sin and its owner, covers the life for protection and supernaturally establishes new ownership. That is the paid-for plan.

The asking becomes the crux of the matter—that's right, free will. In its state of decay and death, where the soul has lost its favor with God, a sincere and remorseful cry activates the compassion of the heart of Jesus Christ, and with loving intercession, He petitions the Father God for the sprinkling of His shed blood from the throne of God to release the soul from the bondage of sin, and restores it to life and health in God. So then, redemption is not a system of exchange but rather a freeing of the soul from the shackles of death, because ownership was not lawfully established, neither is it permanent. Yes, the bondage and the label *sinner* were deeded by trickery—smooth deception of unsuspecting souls, gullible and naïve to the dangers of sin, with wanton desires flaring. That's right, insatiable appetites are the catalysts for spiritual bondage, and death is the ultimate fruit.

Who owns me? There is no way around it; entrance into this world stamped us with the label *sinner.* At the age of accountability—an age I believe that God decides, when mankind consciously begins to reject God and choose sin—we establish the team on which we serve.

Further, as humans we sell our souls to the Devil when blood is shed to serve gods, confer title, satisfy earthly desires, establish control or protection, or any reason that facilitates human greed, desires, or lusts.

Escape to the kingdom of the living God is also confirmed by blood, but that blood is already shed; to enter into the safety and protection of Almighty God, one has to believe and trust the blood that was shed by Jesus Christ on Calvary and by faith, ask for its covering. First, however, there has to be the born-again experience. From whatever angle we take it, bloodshed answers to a higher power.

It is clear that blood is significant to both spiritual kingdoms. Humans know that to take life to another level, sacrifices are made, and when sacrifices are given in the form of blood, we are no longer tampering with mere humanity; we are meddling with spiritual beings. Blood from animals or humans offered as a sacrifice to the Devil awakens the beasts of hell and its master to cement their unrestrictive control over the lives involved. Once that blood enters the throne of hell and is accepted, it unleashes and activates ruthless demons, satisfied and filled with venomous desires to accomplish the task at hand. Blood-satisfied demons, powered by the thrill of death, become ravenous, unstoppable beasts that are let loose into the earth, and their mark leave trails of evil. God has no choice but to honor that act, and He does. Remember the words *free will.*

Ultimately, blood settles ownership, and ownership by blood is honored in the spirit world. God always plays by the rules; therefore, we can be settled in His acknowledgment of those who choose to shed or spill blood to gain worldly affirmation and stature. We also know hell is guided by a lack of ethics; but though the enemy would like to intercept the blood of Christ and ignore its potency and effect, he cannot. Why? Jesus Christ is Lord; we could end the story here. However, to access the blood of Christ is to access redemption. There is no redemption for those who make their bed in hell. Let's take it another mile. The Devil's domain is contrary to holiness; he simply cannot approach, dispute, or disrupt its efficacy. There is no entry or disruption of the presence of holiness, and Christ's blood is holy.

If blood indeed carries life, then each life must carry a significant value in the spirit world. Each life that is taken and drop of blood that is spilled weighs monumentally to the owner of that life. Paul wrote in Romans 6:16 that we are servants of the master to whom we obey; Well, the master of my life defaults as my owner—no questions here! When servants of the Devil die, those lives belong to him; one more unsuspecting soul that finds no rest with its Father God. The enemy benefits from lost souls. When an individual who has committed his or her life to God dies, that life belongs to God for eternity, and God has rewards for those who have conquered the snares and traps set here on earth to bar us from His Presence, humbled and buffeted ourselves in honor of Christ, trusted in God's Word and exited in purity.

For those who have committed their lives to Christ, His blood cleanses and purifies unto righteousness. Romans 6:16 says, "Know ye not, that to whom ye yield yourselves servants to obey, his servants ye are to whom ye obey; whether of sin unto death, or of obedience unto righteousness?"

Righteousness, not goodness, for there is a clear difference between goodness and righteousness. Goodness can be attained by concentrated efforts and by choice. Righteousness is not a human characteristic. It is the character of God given as a free gift to those who have chosen Christ and the plan of salvation. Righteousness is bestowed by God and fueled by grace. Therefore, it is righteousness and not goodness that places man in a God-centered relationship and its ensuing inheritance. Yes, in order for me to profess Jesus Christ as my Lord and Savior, I must be born again.

Jesus answered, "I tell you the truth, no one can enter the kingdom of God unless he is born of water and the Spirit. Flesh gives birth to flesh, but the Spirit gives birth to Spirit. You should not be surprised at my saying, 'You must be born again.' The wind blows wherever it pleases. You hear its sound, but you cannot tell where it comes from or where it is going. So it is with everyone born of the Spirit." (John 3:5–8)

Just being a good person does not activate change of ownership. Obedience to sin gave the enemy control of my life, making me his servant, and changing guards requires more than just good deeds. Spiritual ownership is designated by servanthood, where the exchange must satisfy the masters. Since we were deeded to sin by birth, the change—what I like to call *the escape*—requires the blood of Jesus. What if one becomes dissatisfied with the kingdom of God and wishes to go back to the camp of the enemy? Dear Lord, hell will welcome you with open arms. No, there is no blood requirement—not ever.

Men who choose to dispute the birth of the Lord Jesus Christ, His deity and the sovereignty and existence of God should reconsider. Satan, the enemy of mankind's soul, cannot afford to entertain that notion, or his kingdom would cease to exist. Of course, it is just another sinister lie in his bag of tricks to win another life, but he himself can never indulge. That would be the end of evil here on earth. Those of us who have lived long enough know the Devil is not stupid.

The offering of Christ's blood is why Jesus said in John 14:6, "No man can come to the Father but by me." Then Acts 4:12 says, "Nor is there salvation in any other, for there is no other name under heaven given among men by which we must be saved." To accept Jesus Christ as Lord and Savior is to acknowledge and submit to the legal agreement of the purchase that transpired in the spiritual realm that gives Christ complete authority to be one's Lord and Savior to the end that grace might reign through righteousness and bring about eternal life. Why through Christ's blood? Purity—none other has been found pure in the eyes of God to satisfy the call or the offering of the unblemished sacrifice of blood that was free of sin.

Now the virgin birth makes sense. God, the Creator, needed a sacrificial lamb for mankind. Not a sacrificial animal for man, but the giving of human sacrifice for human redemption. God designed a special creation in the form of His Son. In order not to tamper with the physical laws of earth, this spiritual plan had to be offered to and accepted by a human. We know the Holy Spirit is given to the earth for miracles; that is a spiritual law that is set forth and acceptable for the earth. Spirits can engage man to bring about supernatural miracles. The Virgin Mary accepted the plan when she said, "Be it unto me according to Your Word." (Luke 1:38). The Holy Spirit overshadowed her and implanted the Son of the Lord God inside her. There was no comingling of mother and baby's blood or there would have been a breach and the high possibility of termination of the fetus. So Jesus, the Son of God, was given to the earth and born of a woman (which made Him human), but the holy seed was knowledgeable in all the wisdom of God—Emmanuel, God with us. Jesus then accomplished His life's purpose with the ultimate focus, and offered His blood for the purchase of man from the death of hell.

We cannot cross over into the spiritual realm without blood; taking the hands-off position simply says, *I wish to remain servant to him who owns me.* To have audience with God the Father, I must accept and honor the sacrifice of the shed blood of Jesus Christ. Jesus Christ is the door to the Father God.

CHAPTER 6

Blood as a Covering

To be covered with the blood of Jesus Christ is to be covered with the life of Christ.

In the Garden of Eden, Adam and Eve covered themselves after they sinned. Why? The act of sin automatically uncovers us, strips us of the presence and the glory of God, and then leaves us spiritually unprotected—naked. Only after sin is committed can we feel the spiritual ramifications of the uncovering of the glory of God. The uncovering leaves us bare and an open target to the onslaught and torment of the foes of hell, shame with fear being the burden of the torture.

In order for covering to be restored, there must be atonement. Atonement comes only through blood. Sin, which is disobedience to God's Word and His will, is a spiritual act carried out in the earth, and because it is spiritual, it requires a spiritual payment. Blood is the only covering that satisfies the payment for sin. Blood is the currency of the spirit world. Blood covers the purchased possession, and that indicates ownership. God said, "Whenever I see the blood, I will pass over you," (Genesis 12:13) indicating that the blood has distinctive qualities identified in the spirit world and provides protection or distinction to those it covers.

Blood, then, is the perfect spiritual covering. How do we know this? God killed an animal to cover Adam and Eve after they sinned. God gave a temporary sacrifice for Adam and Eve's sins by offering blood from an animal. In the Old Testament, the shedding of blood came from animals without spot or blemish, signifying purity, innocence, and incorruptibility—the pure for the impure, the clean for the unclean, the whole for the broken, truth restored where deceit was sown. The sacrifice must be free from sin, and the sacrifice must be blood. Adam and Eve covered themselves with leaves, but that was a physical attempt to fix the spiritual problem of sin. Leaves could not restore their status or cover their sins. We know this because they hid from God when He came calling, indicating that the guilt and shame of sin was still present.

Sufficient covering is restorative. God properly covered Adam and Eve when He shed the blood of an animal, and in the spirit, they were adequately covered—atoned for. Atonement is restorative. Animals have no sin, no intellectual nature to render their lives unholy. Man does. Man sins with understanding, whether deceived or not, presumptuous, or drawn by insatiable lust—man sins by choice.

God set in place the use of holy blood to cover sins. Interestingly, the Bible does not offer an explanation for this life-giving substance, as to the reason for its spiritual efficacy or why it was chosen to correlate with the spirit except that it carries life, the breath of God. Therefore, it would be accurate to say that God himself is distributed throughout the earth in each individual. I am a carrier. A bit of God is displayed in the earth through me.

Other intellectually suitable answers can be linked to or mirror the physical functions of blood. Where it establishes a state of equilibrium and provides nutrients for the body, we can also see the life of God, breathed into man with the same function; the function of defense and waste removal can correlate to the covering and protection God provides through the work of redemptive blood. Finally, all things being equal, the blood of Jesus Christ our Lord places us in a state of spiritual health with our Father God.

We know that God formed man from dust, and man, when he dies and is buried, blends once again with dust. In our limited understanding we can grasp that phenomenon. The Bible says that after the image was formed, God breathed into it and it began to live; again, we grasp this concept, because when man dies he gives up that breath, and the frame goes limp.

How about being created in the image of God—what does that mean? Jesus, when He was ready to ascend to the Father, gave Thomas His hands that had the prints of the nails (Luke 24:39), and said, "A spirit has not flesh and bones." Remember, the bones churn out the cells that make blood. Does the glorified body have blood? Jesus constantly reminds us of the resurrection during his teachings, and before His death, He assured His disciples He was going to prepare a place for them, that where He is, there we (who are resurrected in Christ) will be also. Will we have glorified bodies with flesh and bones; will we be able to eat and such to live in that place? Will the children who die in their Lord Christ not be spirits in the hereafter?

Image in its proper context would mean *form,* but in an intended context, it could be extended to mean "containing the innate functional quality to be the offspring of the Creator himself." Jesus, in His glorified body, just prior to ascension, is the picture of "man in the image of God." The resurrected Christ was a man in purity, a man who was no longer vulnerable to the enemy of life, a man who had triumphed over sin and death, a man in unique oneness with His maker in visage and purity indeed.

Is it possible that there is truly a divine connection between God and man, and that there exists a pure Love that binds the heart of man to his

Creator, where even a shamefully brutal sacrifice of the Lord of Glory by mankind could not deter the reconciliation set forth by the will of our Father God? Further, is it possible that there truly is a hell that is ruled by the hater of all flesh, whose sole existence is to cheat man out of the love of Christ?

Again, the angel told Mary, the mother of Jesus, that the holy thing which was conceived in her was of the Holy Spirit, not of man. Therefore, God had preordained that the Holy Thing, Emmanuel, would be God's child, a mysterious implantation, the use of a woman's body to carry holy seed, the spotless answer for the once-and-for-all covering of the sins of mankind. So those who believe and accept Christ's blood as covering for sin are free from the bitterness of the effect and sting of sin.

First Corinthians 15:56–57 says, "The sting of death is sin; and the strength of sin is the law. But thanks be to God, which gives us the victory through our Lord Jesus Christ." Ezekiel 18:20 states, "The soul that sins, it shall die."

Sin automatically removes the presence of God, but it does not remove the love of God.

The enemy is after life. Let's say that again. The enemy is after your blood. Jesus came to give life, and life more abundantly. Jesus Christ came to earth and sacrificed His blood freely so that we might have a protective shield against the darts of hell.

What sacrifice does the enemy make for those who serve him? What has Satan offered to those who have dedicated their time to honoring him? What does he give to those who have spent their time furthering his kingdom? Aren't they still inflicted with the fear and loathsomeness of the sting of sin and death? Let the truth be proclaimed, *he has nothing to offer*. All that man will receive from the hand of evil will be the consolation they see in this life, because Satan is impotent in the spiritual realm. He has but a short time to play his game of deceit, and he plays it well. At the end comes the judgment, and his game will end.

When we accept by faith the blood of Jesus Christ, we partake in the covering and covenant of His love. As we enter into this covenant—again, by faith—God bestows the gift of eternal life. If we forsake Christ's blood, we forsake the covenant, and we forsake life. All that is left is an uncovered spirit that becomes clay for the enemy. When the enemy has your life, he has your blood. That's why many lives are cut short in bloodshed, or why sin ravishes the body and torments the mind until death takes over. Only then is the enemy satisfied; when he has blood, he gains another life.

The holy blood of Christ is reverenced in the spirit world. It is not a commodity that can be ignored or trampled; it is the signature of God upon the life of the chosen. When it is applied as the covering for mankind—whatever or whomever Christ's blood covers—it silences hell and its cohorts.

The plan that God devised to counter the exchange in the Garden of Eden was the atoning blood of a spotless lamb free from the guile or craftiness of sin. Atoning blood of animals continued until a New Testament was written through the life of Jesus Christ. Now the Lamb is the humble, willing heart of God's son. Christ, the Anointed One, became like the first man, Adam. Romans 5:14–21 says, "Through the offence of one man (Adam) came the judgment of death upon all mankind." Even without the consciousness of sin, we became heirs to the design of a devious plot and a battle for our very lives.

Abba Father, the beginning and the end, initiated a new strategy midstream by sending His only begotten Son, Christ Jesus, who was full of grace and truth. By Christ's righteousness—the righteousness of one man—a gift was offered for those who choose not to accept the death sentence handed down from Adam. The even exchange of life for life (the gift of Christ's spotless offering of His life) had to be accepted by the enemy. Why? Satan called the shot of *sin upon all* by deceiving the first man and all his offspring. Now Jesus Christ, whose blood was not of Adam's vein—for Mary was impregnated by the overshadowing of the Holy Spirit—was free from the label *sinner;* therefore, Christ's blood was the perfect offering, the perfect exchange for a sinful life. He now calls the shot of redemption for whosoever believes in Him.

How is blood identified in the spirit realm? Blood types are one of the kinds of marker systems that a mammalian body uses to identify its cells. This is important because mammals have a marvelous group of organs called the immune system. The immune system is designed to identify cells and other objects that are foreign or innate to the body. However, if the armies of the immune system (composed of an incredible group of proteins called antibodies) cannot identify the cells that belong to the body, they will destroy the body's cells right along with the invaders.

Our blood cells have markers on their surfaces, and our immune systems have learned to accept the body's cells and attack cells with foreign markers on them. Transfused blood type A is not mixed with blood type B, and so forth; the immune system would attack and destroy the A cells, which would not only make the transfusion worthless, but also would create catastrophic problems from the increased breakdown of material produced by the destruction of all those A cells introduced during the transfusion.

Is it the purity or impurity of blood that is recognized in the spirit, or is there a spiritual mark on blood? Is the covering of the blood of Christ a sort of a spiritual cloak, or does it provide divine angelic protection over those who have accepted its offering? Is the covering activated through the born-again theory recorded in the Gospel of John, creating a new spiritual man? (It does read "born again of the Spirit.") Could covering mean the deposit of the life of Christ in those who ask for His blood? Looking through the eyes of the Spirit, are those who have been born again hidden in God through Christ?

I am crucified with Christ: nevertheless I live; yet not I, but Christ lives in me: and the life which I now live in the flesh I live by the faith of the Son of God, who loved me, and gave himself for me. (Galatians 2:20)

And be found in him, not having mine own righteousness, which is of the law, but that which is through the faith of Christ, the righteousness which is of God by faith: That I may know him, and the power of his resurrection, and the fellowship of his sufferings, being made conformable unto his death. (Philippians 3:9–10)

In Him, the born-again are tucked away under the wings of their Lord, sanctified, and made heirs of the inheritance according to the eternal purpose of God the Father so that the purchased possession who believe by faith should become partakers of the promise! Then all glory and honor to Him who is able to do exceedingly abundantly above all we can ask or think, because His power works in us—all glory be to Him, forever and ever.

CHAPTER 7

Blood Speaks

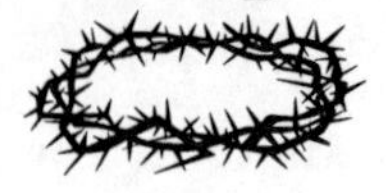

The enemy has made no sacrifice for man. Instead, he uses the blood sacrifice of defenseless animals or brother against brother.

So far, we have established that blood is alive, blood redeems, and blood covers; now comes the premise that blood speaks. If all this is true, then this tissue is not merely a necessary component of the anatomy. No other tissue, organ, or system alone has earned the credence of blood. Some organs, like the liver, can function on as low as 30 percent capacity; others can be removed without tremendous effects on the body; but as soon as the blood cell count is lowered, it begins to speak. When the doctor says the cell count is low, there is cause for great concern, and the emphasis is on how to raise them back to normal levels.

Beyond its physical tones, blood has a spiritual voice. Man does not have the ability to hear blood audibly, but it sure weighs on the conscience of those beguiled into its spiritual misuse. Switch realms, and blood speaks.

In Genesis 4, the sons of Adam and Eve brought their gifts and made a presentation to God. God accepted Abel's offering but not Cain's. The rejection of the gift was so intolerable to Cain that he rose up in anger and killed his brother. The Lord God came to Cain and asked,

"Where is Abel, your brother?" And Cain said, "I know not: Am I my brother's keeper?" And God said, "What have you done? The voice of your brother's blood cries unto me from the ground. You are cursed from the earth, which has opened her mouth to receive your brother's blood from your hand." God heard the cry of Abel's blood and responded to the cry by cursing Cain. Cain became a fugitive and a vagabond in the earth after the curse; his skill was wasted, not producing for him anymore. The earth and its treasures became illusive, like a shadow to the man. Literally, he aimlessly occupied space on the earth until his death.

Bloodshed has become a normal part of man's livelihood. It is natural to hunt or domesticate animals and kill them for food. The purpose of shedding blood makes all the difference. In Leviticus 17, God outlined His command on this matter to Moses. "Whoever kills an ox, or lamb, or goat (in the camp or outside the camp) and does not bring it to the door of the Tabernacle as an offering to the Lord, that the Priest may sprinkle the blood upon the altar, and burn the fat for a sweet savor unto the Lord, has offered this blood to devils after whom they are lusting for the treasures and bounty of the earth. That person will be held responsible for the shed blood and I will cut him off from his people. This will become a law forever and will be to strangers or anyone that comes among you. Do not offer burnt offerings or sacrifices of blood or I the Lord God will set my face against that soul that eats or sacrifices blood unto devils."

Leviticus 17:11 says, "For the life of the flesh is in the blood: and I have given it to you upon the altar to make an atonement for your souls: for it is the blood that makes an atonement for the soul."

David was King of Israel, a man chosen by God for a great task. During his reign, David decided to build a temple for the Lord God of Israel, but God told King David not to build Him a temple, because he had blood on his hands. First Chronicles 28:3 says, "But God said unto me, Thou shall not build a house for my name, because thou hast been a man of war, and hast shed blood." Here is part of the story. King David, taking a stroll on his roof top one day, laid eyes on a beautiful woman taking a bath, and he wanted her; had to have her; did not stop until she was in his bed. He discovered that she was married, but that did not deter his passion. Instead, he ordered the woman's husband killed so he could freely indulge.

The Bible speaks of this king as a man after God's own heart. Many of the Psalms or songs of praise were written by him, and it is obvious that this king sought to live for God. Failure of this magnitude—especially recorded in the archives and handed down to us—must carry a noteworthy message. Though David repented, the stench of blood spoke in the nostrils of God. King David had a vision for a temple to be built in Jerusalem in honor of his God. What an awesome vision he must have had for that glorious temple. It seems as if this temple would have marked a significant achievement in the life of this king, but the lot fell to his son. Today, lots of people refer to King David and his achievements, but the glory of one of the greatest temples built on earth is attributed to his son, Solomon.

By now, we have been familiarized with many stories of the Bible. Here is another. In the land of Ur of the Chaldeans, God called a man named Abraham and began to speak with him as a man would speak to his friend. God told Abraham that He would bless Abraham's loins so that Abraham would become a great nation. Further, God took Abraham away from his people and continued to instruct him on how to become a nation exclusive to God, with laws, rituals, a land they would call home, and a special covenant. This covenant between God and His friend was made by blood. God told Abraham to remove the foreskin of every male child born to him—blood ownership. This blood ritual established an everlasting covenant between God and Abraham's seed (the Jewish nation) perpetually. God would be their God, and the token of circumcision became the covenant between them.

And I will establish my covenant between Me and you and your seed after you in their generations for an everlasting covenant, to be a God unto you, and to your seed after you. And I will give unto you, and to your seed after you, the land wherein you are a stranger, all the land of Canaan, for an everlasting possession; and I will be their God. And God said unto Abraham, You shall keep My covenant therefore, you, and your seed after you in their generations. This is My covenant, which you shall keep, between Me and you and your seed after you; every male child among you shall be circumcised. And you shall circumcise the flesh of your foreskin; and it shall be a token of the covenant betwixt Me and you. (Genesis 17:7–11)

Clearly, blood carries a mark in the spirit. In this ritual, the symbolism establishes the rights of a nation to a Holy God. Isn't it marvelous to know that by choice and subsequent obedience, we are distinguished to enter the Presence of the Lord God Almighty?

Many years later, the children of Abraham's seed became slaves to the Egyptians. This bondage was no ordinary matter. An entire nation was enslaved until God ordained blood. The first plague against Egypt on behalf of the children of Israel was blood.

And the Lord spoke unto Moses, "Say unto Aaron, 'Take thy rod and stretch out your hand upon the waters of Egypt, upon their streams, upon their rivers, and upon their ponds, and upon all their pools of water, that they may become blood; and that there may be blood throughout all the land of Egypt, both in vessels of wood and in vessels of stone.'" (Exodus 7:19)

Indulge my speculation. Could this plague be symbolic of the blood of those who died at the cruelty of the hands of Pharaoh—over four hundred years of blood rising up, crying, bringing a stench, bringing thirst, destroying the food supply, tormenting the minds of the living, wreaking havoc on the land, speaking its language in earthly tones, crying "Death, death, death?"

The process of deliverance from slavery was carried out in phases. One after another, plagues were poured out on the land of Egypt until God was ready to release the Israelites completely from bondage. However, we cannot miss this important cue; the last plague on the land of Egypt was not commanded until atonement through a spotless lamb was made. Before God shows His glory, before He fulfills His promise, before God brings us into our desired heaven, before God answers the wailing of the soul, He ordains blood.

And Moses said, "Thus says the Lord, 'About midnight will I go out into the midst of Egypt: and all the firstborn in the land of Egypt shall die, from the firstborn of Pharaoh that sits upon his throne, even unto the firstborn of the maidservant that is behind the mill; and all the firstborn of beasts. And there shall be a great cry throughout all the land of Egypt, such as there was none like it, nor shall be like it any more. But against any of the children of Israel shall not a dog move his tongue, against man or beast: that ye may know how that the Lord doth put a difference between the Egyptians and Israel.'" (Exodus 11:4–7)

Never before had God given such a mandate. Blood filled the land in the beginning, and blood filled the land at the end. The currency of the spirit was sufficiently offered and received. The invoice was stamped, "paid in full." That night, God crushed Pharaoh's spirit with a death blow, and crushed his empire by taking the heir, the seed, the hope of Egypt, and other possible heirs who were eligible to reign and carry on the inherited legacy. Not only that, but God recompensed Pharaoh for his unthinkable act of killing the male children at the time Moses was born.

Before the Exodus came the Passover; a holy sacrifice of a spotless lamb, chosen and precious, dear to the Father's heart, given as a free gift of love for a wounded people—a people without strength, a broken people. To rise up from the ash of defeat, there needs to be the offering and the receipt of blood—pure, holy, unblemished and free of sin. A holy covenant of blood, made by those in need to a holy God.

God's instructions were clear. He told Moses to speak to all the congregation of Israel, saying, "In the tenth day of this month they will take every man a lamb, according to the house of their fathers, a lamb for each house." (Exodus 12:3). The lamb chosen was to be without blemish and a male of the first year. It could be taken from the sheep or from the goats, and the people were to keep it until the fourteenth day of the same month. After the fellowship with this chosen lamb, the whole assembly of the congregation of Israel was instructed to kill it in the evening, take of the blood, and strike it on the two side posts and upper door post of the houses in the same homes that they ate. Further, they were to eat it in haste, with their loins girded, shoes on their feet and staffs in their hands—a preparation for the Exodus. It was the Lord's Passover. Then the Lord continued, "For I will pass through the land of Egypt this night, and will smite all the firstborn in the land of Egypt, both man and beast; and against all the gods of Egypt I will execute judgment: I am the Lord." (Exodus 12:12)

The common thread here in the language of blood is the revenge for the weak from God, who heard the cry of the slain. Amen! We can lift our heads in confidence, knowing that God's ears are not deaf that He cannot hear, His hands are not shortened that He cannot save, and He is a defender of the defenseless.

But let's stand in the shoes of the Cains, the King Davids and the Pharaohs of the world. What circumstances impale themselves upon mankind, leaving us in the throes of darkness so that without compassion for the sanctity of life, we can commit the act of slaying each other? How do we free ourselves from the talons and vices of death that both enslave and mockingly cry against us? Jesus told the crowd, "Come unto me all you who labor and are heavy laden and I will give you rest. Take my yoke upon you, and learn of me...for my yoke is easy and my burden is light." (Matthew 11:28-30) And in Hebrews 12, we are entreated to come to Jesus, the mediator of the new covenant, and to His blood of sprinkling that speaks better things than that of Abel. Jesus Christ will make a covenant with the whomsoever will, if only they seek Him with all their hearts.

CHAPTER 8

Spirit, Water, and Blood

For whosoever is born of God overcomes the world.
—1 John 5:4

The spiritual relevance of water is a phenomenon that must be explained in truth to gain its heavenly perspective. Water is indispensable throughout the world, in every culture, for recreation, food, health, industry, agriculture, and cleansing. Water is also part of an important symbolic religious ritual used extensively by the followers of Christ and in other religious beliefs.

What is water? More than 70 percent of the earth is covered in water. More than 60 percent of the body's content is water. Amniotic fluid is water; spinal fluid is water; tears are water; saliva, mucus, and lymph contain water. Forty percent of the cells contain water, but most significantly, 55 percent of blood is water. There is just a sense that water has utmost importance, but its abundance may have caused us to demean or overlook its value.

The inauguration of Jesus' ministry on earth took place by baptism in the river Jordan. Each gospel writer of the New Testament was also careful to document the baptism of Jesus by water, specifying its utter importance. John the Baptist immersed Jesus in water, and as He came up out of the water, the Spirit of God descended upon Him, and a declaration was heard by those around as God announced, "This is My beloved Son in whom I am well pleased." (Matthew 3:17)

Here is the sequence. Jesus' ministry started with water, after which the Holy Spirit descended upon Him, and at the close of His life was the offering of His blood. Neither the Bible nor history gives record of much of Jesus' life between the ages of twelve and the time of His baptism. However, after the initiation in water, the documented life of His ministry began. Water baptism signified the beginning.

Baptism, as it has been handed down to us, has taken on different meanings to different denominations. However, the Bible tells us in Galatians 3 that as many as are baptized into Christ have put on Christ. It is further clarified in Colossians 2 that the believer is buried with Christ in baptism, and then raised with Him through faith by the mysterious work of God. Baptism, then, is the spiritual burial of the inner man, and the rising up of a spiritually sanctified new man who is covered in Christ. We who have been baptized in Christ are spiritually covered in, not by, the protection of His being. The process makes the believer alive in Christ with sins forgiven. Any contrary ordinance that may have stood against that person is blotted out. Then comes the disarming of principalities and powers to the end that those in Christ may experience triumphant victory—the raising up of that new spiritual man who is born again.

In St. John 3, the story is told of Nicodemus, a Jewish ruler who came to Jesus, inquiring of His miraculous power. In the conversation, Jesus told him, "You must be born again; that is, born of water and of the Spirit." Again in 1 John 5:6, John tells his readers, "There are three that bear witness in heaven: the Father, the Word, and the Holy Spirit; and these three are one. And there are three that bear witness on earth: the Spirit, the water, and the blood; and these three agree as one." There appears, then, to be an indispensable relationship on the earth of Spirit, water, and blood, and the three in union transmit strategic signals in the spirit.

Examination of the tissues of the body leaves us in awe, as we recognize that they are all immersed or suspended in water, saturated by blood and controlled by the spirit of man—for without the spirit, the body is dead. Jesus and His followers were immersed in water baptism, then John explained the phenomenon of a mysterious agreement that conceived oneness. Water and blood work like a completed electrical circuit that begins to function when plugged into the socket of the spirit.

So then, intrinsic to all human beings are the criteria, the embodiment, the mystery of a spiritual empowerment for knowledge and wisdom of the Spirit, which includes purification and cleansing for a seamless connection—all are covered in the blood, which secures the union that lies within us through obedience to the requirements of Christ's new covenant. Thoughts, words, and deeds can lead us in directions opposite to the pure nature of God. The constant need for repentance to maintain the seamless connection is merely an understanding of the God-natured purity we ought to possess. After we have been baptized in Christ, there is the availability of washing by the Word that continues to work for our cleansing.

Ephesians 5:25–27 states, "Husbands, love your wives, even as Christ also loved the Church, and gave Himself for it; that He might sanctify and cleanse it with the washing of water by the Word; that He might present it to Himself a glorious Church, not having spot, or wrinkle, or any such thing; but that it should be holy and without blemish."

Continuous cleansing! For every religious ritual requiring baptism—which for some is immersion in water, and for others is the sprinkling of water—the same idea of continuous cleansing is true. Meaning, just as baptism in Christ washes us clean of the deeds of past sins or past involvement that is not of Christ, so baptism unto any other group washes the individual clean of the involvement in any previous religion, and sets him or her apart unto that religion into which he or she is baptized.

It is commonly known that a visit to the voodoo priest or witchdoctor requires a washing. For the ritual to be effective, the seeker has to be washed of any past religious involvement—especially of the power of Christ. The work of the crucified Savior, Jesus Christ, must be washed away in order for the work of darkness to take its course.

When the Roman soldiers were ready to take their victims from the cross at the time of Jesus' crucifixion, a lance was used to pierce Jesus' side, and blood and water, distinctly separate, flowed from the puncture. Medical speculations conclude that the buildup of fluid in the pleural cavity, incurred due to the hemorrhaging from continuous beatings, could have caused serum and blood particles to separate, yielding what has been written as "blood and water flowing from His side." Was this another important clue to the significance of the mystery of Spirit, water, and blood, which fulfill the criteria on earth to write the connection of unity of the born-again to their God within the spiritual realm? Was this a divine symbolic execution of the melding of earth to heaven? Then as the born-again are united with Christ the Word, they are pulled into the unity of the agreement of heaven through the Spirit.

It is significant that John, in his revelation of this spiritual truth, saw Christ as the Word, not as a savior, a judge, or even love. So those who are immersed in the Word—as the Word is the truth of God—are those who are plugged into this divine unity. This mystery leaves no room for the born-again to establish their own order, convictions, or beliefs; the divine foundation of this God-centered unity is already established. Baptism, according to Paul's letter to the Colossians, signifies the burial of the physical man, and the rising up of a quickened man, a new spiritual man, able to attain to the realms of the Spirit. And as Jesus, who paved the way for us through the shedding of His blood, triumphed over the principalities and powers of hell, so now those who have been risen with Him in baptism, and seated in heavenly places in Christ, are empowered to rule over the forces of darkness by the Spirit of God who testifies to the new birth in those who have been purified through baptism.

Just prior to the revelation of the agreement of Spirit, water, and blood on earth, John wrote that He who overcomes the world, the system, the clauses set out to trap the heart of man, is he who believes and therefore lives by the footprints of Jesus, the Son of God. It is amazing that the truth and glory of God are at our fingertips with complete access found in the simplicity of obedience.

CHAPTER 9

God Speaks on the Abominations of Blood

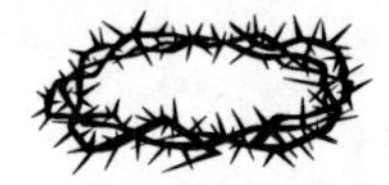

> You shall not bring an abomination into your house, lest you be doomed to destruction like it. You shall utterly detest it and utterly abhor it, for it is an accursed thing.
> —Deuteronomy 7:26

Again the Word of the Lord came unto me, saying, Son of man, cause Jerusalem to know her abominations ... And as for your nativity, in the day you were born your navel was not cut, neither were you washed in water to supple you; you were not salted at all, nor swaddled at all. No eye pitied you, to do any of these unto you, to have compassion upon you; but you were cast out in the open field, to the loathing of your person, in the day that you were born. And when I passed by you, and saw you polluted in your own blood, I said unto you when you were in your blood, "Live"; yes, I said unto you when you were in your blood, "Live." (Ezekiel 16:1–6)

The Old Testament prophet Ezekiel lived around the time of 622 to 600 BC. He was from the land of Judah but was taken captive and exiled to Babylon during the first raid of King Nebuchadnezzar. His prophetic words came to the house of Israel, the false prophets, the elders, the priests and leaders of the Hebrew nation, as the people had strayed from the principles of their God. The prophetic word reveals a sort of otherworld-like glory that requires expressive imagination, yet it clearly defines the persona of God to His people.

To identify the state of the house at the time of this prophecy, the people of Samaria were given the name Aholah, which translates "her tent or idolatrous sanctuary," while the people of Jerusalem were given the symbolic name Aholibah, which means "my tent." We could add our own interpretation to these names. *Her tent* and *my tent* could possibly mean the establishing of her laws or my laws instead of God's law. Further, in Ezekiel chapter 2, the people were called rebellious and stiff-hearted transgressors. The message Ezekiel brought was a warning to save the people from the horror of a pending doom, the consequence of establishing their own laws which resulted in abominations to their God.

So great was the defilement of God's people that God equated it to the pollution of baking food with human dung. Imagine the stench. Imagine the horror of sitting down to that meal. Such were the requirements on the prophet Ezekiel to communicate the warning so that God's people would begin to perceive, not understand, as to understand the holiness of God would require a God-sense, but in limited human reasoning, they would have an idea of the extent to which they had nauseated the Holy One and the fierceness of the wrath about to be poured out.

It would not be redundant to repeat that this message was for the people of God, the called, the chosen, the priests and the leaders of the Church. Too many of us choose to call upon God in times of need yet neglect to honor God with our lives and to be called by His name—until, of course, we approach His throne again to petition His hand. This word was for a nation— a people who knew God but limited their involvement to convenience.

The King James translation of the Bible tells us that God was against the altars and images and idols of the high places. Altars were built in elevated regions, like hills or mountains, and blood sacrifices were made on these altars to various gods. Ezekiel 6:9 says, "I am broken with their whorish heart, which has departed from me, and with their eyes, which go a whoring after their idols: and they shall loathe themselves for the evils which they have committed in all their abomination."

This message is followed by the indicator of the corresponding result in Chapter 7, where the land was full of bloody crimes and the city full of violence. Destruction came, and the people searched for peace and found none. The Word of God perished from the priest, and wise council was not found in the elders.

In Chapter 8, Ezekiel was shown abominable drawings or symbols on the wall of the court with women weeping after a strange god, and in the Lord's house, men sat worshiping the sun yet turned their backs on God. The very next verse, (17) shows that the land was filled with violence because of these abominations.

Violence in the land stems from man's irreverence to God. The pattern is, disregarding God first and then having contempt for one another. When mankind is brazen enough to talk against God, turn their backs on God and clearly make the choice to serve their idols while blatantly disrespecting the holiness of the Lord God Almighty, will they find it in their hearts to respect each other? Doesn't violence come naturally when moral guidelines are fuzzy? If I have no reverential fear or sense of awe for the holiness and purity of the Almighty God and His Word, who or what can restrain me from the spirit of evil—the insanity that comes to push me over the edge?

Ezekiel 16 correlates with chapters 22 and 23. The Bride of Christ, after being adorned to perfection, trusted so loftily in her own beauty, and fame, and ability, that she celebrated her rise with harlotry. How did she portray her blessings? She used the gifts given by God and arrayed them before those from whom she sought acceptance, favor and validation; and she offered her children as sacrifices to be eaten and burned by fire. In all this, the Bride—the blessed of the Lord—continued to excel in her blessings while "opening her feet to everyone that passed by and multiplied her whoredoms."

And your elder sister is Samaria, she and her daughters that dwell at your left hand: and your younger sister, that dwells at your right hand, is Sodom and her daughters. Yet you have not walked after their ways, nor done after their abominations: but, as if that were a very little thing, you were corrupted more than they in all your ways. (Ezekiel 16:46–47)

How much more corruption was added to the abomination—to the sin that brought doomed destruction and curses? Adding to the abomination were children who cursed or belittled their mothers and fathers, natives who oppressed strangers and ill-treated the fatherless and widows, people who despised the things of God and showed no respect for the Sabbath, men who devised lies to commit murder, those who uncovered their father's nakedness, and humbled women who were ceremonially unclean at the time of their periods or at the time of childbirth.

And one has committed abomination with his neighbor's wife; and another has lewdly defiled his daughter-in-law; and another has humbled his sister, his father's daughter. You have taken gifts to shed blood; you have taken usury and increase, and you have greedily gained of your neighbors by extortion, and have forgotten me, says the Lord God. Therefore, I beat my fists at the dishonest profit you have made and at the bloodshed which has been in your midst. Can your heart endure, or can your heart remain strong in the days when I shall deal with you? I, the Lord, have spoken, and will do it. (Ezekiel 22:11–14)

They have committed adultery, and blood is in their hands, and with their idols have they committed adultery, and have also caused their sons, whom they bare unto me, to pass for them through the fire, to devour them. Moreover this they have done unto me: they have defiled my sanctuary in the same day, and have profaned my Sabbaths. For when they had slain their children to their idols, then they came the same day into my sanctuary to profane it; and, lo, thus have they done in the midst of mine house. And the righteous men, they shall judge them after the manner of adulteresses, and after the manner of women that shed blood; because they are adulteresses, and blood is in their hands. (Ezekiel 23:37–45)

The whoredom mentioned is both literal and symbolic. It is symbolic in that it epitomizes intimacy with other gods and idols, transcends disloyalty and screams comingled corruption of the holy and the unholy. Cause is established as the harlot is attracted to the glamour customary of the prince of the world, but she elevates her lewdness with unthinkable vulgarity, replacing the purity of the Bride of Christ with insatiable acts of lust as she is sucked into deplorable scum.

Considering the efficacy and potency of the blood of the Passover to Jerusalem, God's chosen people, and also considering the diligence established for this ritual, why didn't the observance of the Passover prevent the captivity of this God-chosen people? If blood truly has a spiritual effect, it must have played a role in the eventuality of this Nation. How did a Nation send such a loathsome message to its God despite its diligent obedience to that which activated, in time past, such a mighty deliverance? There is a sense that these questions contradict and yet answer themselves.

Conscientious commitment to a ritual causes it to lose its effectiveness in matters of holiness and godliness when man's heart is drawn away from God. It is commitment to God that connects the heart, soul, and body to the divinity of God, not dutiful obligation to the ritual. The bloodshed and whoredom Ezekiel mentioned clearly violated the laws of holiness; therefore, participation in the Passover must have been a comingled pollution rather than a celebration of the greatness of God's work. The question can compellingly be answered. Abominations nullify the work of holy blood.

Literally, harlotry violates the principles of blood, as stated clearly in the prophecy of Ezekiel. Mortals are twisted out of natural proportions and take on spirits of jealousy, suicide, hate, murder, and such when betrayed by fornication and adultery. The pungency of the sin creates a despicable taste against the violator, and it does not take a stretch of the imagination for enemies to be born and nurtured for life. In the eyes of a holy God, betrayal by the sin of exchanging intimacy for gain is multiplied by even greater powers.

Further reading in the book of Ezekiel reveals more and more lewdness, as the prophet continues to show the nation her sin. Amidst the scum of evil that is sprawled on the pages of this book, God reveals the sentence of death to come and warning after warning for the land that had departed from its God.

I compared other prophets of the Old Testament (Isaiah, Zechariah and Amos) with the voice of Ezekiel, and scattered throughout the message of these other prophets is a glimmer of hope. Sometimes these prophets catch a glimpse of the reign of the Messiah, and comfort is established in their message. However, with Ezekiel, his glimpse is of the fall of Lucifer. It sends the quivering emphasis that the heart of Lucifer is wrapped securely around those who have extended themselves beyond sin and onto the path of abomination.

First, Lucifer was called the Prince of Tyrus, who was in Eden, the garden of God. (*Tyrus* means "rock" and may carry a reference to the many beautiful stones that adorned this angel.) God told Ezekiel that because Lucifer had lifted up his heart by saying, "I am a God; I sit in the seat of God, in the midst of the seas," he would be cast out as profane out of the mountain of God and be destroyed from the midst of the stones of fire. Then God described the physical beauty of Lucifer, Son of the Morning. He was covered with every precious gemstone—sardius, topaz, diamond, beryl, onyx, jasper, sapphire, emerald, carbuncle, and gold; tambourines and pipes were prepared especially for him. Beyond this musical gift, he was an anointed cherub that protected. God decorated this angel and set him upon the holy mountain of God, where he walked in the midst of the stones of fire. This angel was perfect before the Lord until iniquity was found in his heart. It is relevant to ask the question, "In the midst of perfection and holiness, how did Lucifer breed iniquity; what was its source?" Pride. Lucifer extended his heart to pride, then his beauty and brightness corrupted his wisdom.

This is worth a pause. Pride distorted Lucifer's vision and caused his godly wisdom to change into a stench before God; his wisdom became corruption. There in the midst of heaven, Lucifer became puffed up with pride, began to traffic a multitude of iniquity and filled himself with violence. God told him, "I will cast you to the ground, lay you before kings, and bring a fire from out of you that shall devour you; then I will bring you to ashes upon the earth in the sight of all them that behold you."

The character of this fallen angel still beguiles mankind. The sense of protection is still offered to Lucifer's followers, though he has no foundation from which to deliver this protection. But then, who is he protecting man from? Further, Lucifer's display of pride, flashy styles, and flamboyancy now captivates the hearts of those who serve him, even if honor is devalued to maintain these attributes; and did you note the trafficking of iniquity with violence?

The challenge God offered by Ezekiel's message was not to a class or sect of the nation or to certain communities so that those in elite standing or of higher stature could frown at the lower-classed abominators. The entire nation had come under the guile of the fumes of these abominations. Those who had not strayed into whoredom were not exempt from the violence that reared its ugly head; the darkness was all around. There is nothing symbolic about the darkness of evil. God mandated His priests, leaders, prophets, and people with the directive of watchmen, and saddled them with the responsibility of the vigil of prayer and holiness so that "men may lead a quiet and peaceable life." (1 Timothy 2:2)

If leaders fail, followers are doomed. Failure at the top is a sinister design that undermines the core values and purity of any entity and the ensuing result does not always end in extinction, as the greatest demise is not destruction, but the conversion of the overthrown to serve the conqueror.

The soul that sins, it shall die. But if the wicked will turn from all his sins that he has committed, and keep all my statutes, and do that which is lawful and right, he shall surely live, he shall not die. For I have no pleasure in the death of him that dies, says the Lord God: wherefore turn yourselves, and live. (Ezekiel 18:20–21, 32)

In his final chapters, Ezekiel's vision was of the restoration of the temple to its rightful state of holiness, with healing waters flowing from it to the streets. Again, the message is clear; it is with the gathering of the holy saints that God has commanded His blessings. Therefore, the Church must lead the path to holiness.

CHAPTER 10

Violations of Blood

When wisdom enters your heart, and knowledge is pleasant unto your soul; Discretion shall preserve you, understanding shall keep you. —Proverbs 2:10–11

At any given time and for various reasons, we encounter the use of the living, breathing substance called blood, and sometimes with limited understanding, our involvement stimulates the gates of the spirit and initiates earthly responses. One thing is sure, the misuse of blood triggers haunting repercussions, and though they often escape our awareness, it does not change the bed of needles on which the violators rest. Let's ponder desecrated uses of blood and their corresponding earthly repercussions.

Blood for food: the Lord God uncompromisingly forbids the eating of blood for food.

Whatever man of the children of Israel, or of the strangers who dwell among you, who hunts and catches any animal or bird that may be eaten, he shall pour out its blood and cover it with dust; for it is the life of all flesh. Its blood sustains its life. Therefore I said to the children of Israel, "You shall not eat the blood of any flesh, for the life of all flesh is its blood. Whoever eats it shall be cut off." (Leviticus 17:13–15)

Blood of a virgin: there is something pure and delicate about the eyes of the soul of a virtuous girl. Please note that this is not the girl who has compromised her virtuous standards yet retained parts of her body untouched. Just as a virgin's body is undefiled, so is her mind, and it becomes hard for her to fathom the wiles of the dark spirits that would betray her trust. In the purest sense, she is truly vulnerable and must be protected. So naïve is she that there is almost a sense of trust that the violator would have mercy and not desecrate her. Dishonoring a virtuous girl is equal to wreaking havoc upon every child that her womb produces. The beauty, dignity, and royalty of entering into a joyous marital relationship and producing children are robbed when virtue is stolen. As a result, what she produces in marriage is flawed, needing reassurance that goes beyond the capacity of earthly consolers.

If any man takes a wife, and goes in to her, and detests her, and charges her with shameful conduct, and brings a bad name on her, and says, "I took this woman, and when I came to her I found she was not a virgin," then the father and mother of the young woman shall take and bring out the evidence of the young woman's virginity to the elders of the city at the gate. And the young woman's father shall say to the elders, "I gave my daughter to this man as wife, and he detests her. Now he has charged her with shameful conduct, saying, 'I found your daughter was not a virgin,' and yet these are the evidences of my daughter's virginity." And they shall spread the cloth before the elders of the city. Then the elders of that city shall take that man and punish him; and they shall fine him one hundred shekels of silver and give them to the father of the young woman, because he has brought a bad name on a virgin of Israel. And she shall be his wife; he cannot divorce her all his days. But if the thing is true, and evidences of virginity are not found for the young woman, then they shall bring out the young woman to the door of her father's house, and the men of her city shall stone her to death with stones, because she has done a disgraceful thing in Israel, to play the harlot in her father's house. So you shall put away the evil from among you. (Deuteronomy 22:13–21)

Blood of incest: the Word of the Lord is clear on the matter of incest. None of you shall approach anyone who is near of kin to him, to uncover his nakedness: I am the Lord. The nakedness of your father or the nakedness of your mother you shall not uncover. She is your mother; you shall not uncover her nakedness. The nakedness of your father's wife you shall not uncover; it is your father's nakedness. The nakedness of your sister, the daughter of your father, or the daughter of your mother, whether born at home or elsewhere, their nakedness you shall not uncover. The nakedness of your son's daughter or your daughter's daughter, their nakedness you shall not uncover; for theirs is your own nakedness. The nakedness of your father's wife's daughter, begotten by your father—she is your sister—you shall not uncover her nakedness. You shall not uncover the nakedness of your father's sister; she is near of kin to your father. You shall not uncover the nakedness of your mother's sister, for she is near of kin to your mother. You shall not uncover the nakedness of your father's brother. You shall not approach his wife; she is your aunt. You shall not uncover the nakedness of your daughter-in-law—she is your son's wife—you shall not uncover her nakedness. You shall not uncover the nakedness of your brother's wife; it is your brother's nakedness. You shall not uncover the nakedness of a woman and her daughter, nor shall you take her son's daughter or her daughter's daughter, to uncover her nakedness. They are near of kin to her. It is wickedness. Nor shall you take a woman as a rival to her sister, to uncover her nakedness while the other is alive. (Leviticus 18:6–18)

Blood of menstrual flow and more: during the time of a woman's menstrual flow, her reproductive organs are tender and sensitive to touch. Penetration of any object renders these areas susceptible to absorption, placing the body's immunity at risk. It becomes a premier site to introduce foreign antibodies, which show up later in blood incompatibilities and allergies.

Also you shall not approach a woman to uncover her nakedness as long as she is in her customary impurity. Moreover you shall not lie carnally with your neighbor's wife, to defile yourself with her. And you shall not let any of your descendants pass through the fire to Molech, nor shall you profane the name of your God: I am the Lord. You shall not lie with a male as with a woman. It is an abomination. Nor shall you mate with any animal, to defile yourself with it. Nor shall any woman stand before an animal to mate with it. It is perversion. (Leviticus 18:19–23)

Blood of abortion: I wish we could take an honest survey of the residual pain and devastation that lives beyond the abortion table. Proportionately, the horror of abortion is relatively 10 percent for the unborn and 90 percent for the parties involved in the taking and sacrificing of the life. Indeed, some of us have been desensitized by the corruption of capital gain, but others live with blood crying in our ears and against us like nightmares of invisible stalkers. The haunting feelings attract a certain caliber of unwholesome, perverted individuals to our attention, and mask us from the purity of sound, healthy, lasting relationships. Death seems to lurk inside the womb and attaches itself to the souls that are formed thereafter, leaving victims who become prone to accidents, tragedies, and weird kinds of failures. Anger takes a seat at the mother's door, betrayal rides her skirt, and a sense of "I deserve this" leaves her taunted by life's mishaps.

For it was You who created my inward parts; You knit me together in my mother's womb. I will praise You because I have been remarkably and wonderfully made. Your works are wonderful, and I know this very well. My bones were not hidden from You when I was made in secret, when I was formed in the depths of the earth. Your eyes saw me when I was formless; all my days were written in Your book and planned before a single one of them began. (Psalm 139:13–16, HCSB)

Blood of murder: The loss of a life to the violence of murder ranks highly with one of the greatest pain mankind endures. Loved ones enduring the loss continue life with an emptiness of the soul and an inconsolable sob that can be triggered by even a sound.

It came to pass that Cain brought an offering of the fruit of the ground to the Lord. Abel also brought of the firstborn of his flock and of their fat. And the Lord respected Abel and his offering, but He did not respect Cain and his offering. And Cain was very angry, and his countenance fell. So the Lord said to Cain, "Why are you angry? And why has your countenance fallen? If you do well, will you not be accepted? And if you do not do well, sin lies at the door. And its desire is for you, but you should rule over it." Now Cain talked with Abel his brother; and it came to pass, when they were in the field, that Cain rose up against Abel his brother and killed him. Then the Lord said to Cain, "Where is Abel your brother?" He said, "I do not know. Am I my brother's keeper?" And He said, "What have you done? The voice of your brother's blood cries out to Me from the ground. So now you are cursed from the earth, which has opened its mouth to receive your brother's blood from your hand. When you till the ground, it shall no longer yield its strength to you. A fugitive and a vagabond you shall be on the earth." (Genesis 4:3–12)

Blood of tribal rituals: rituals are based on the belief of satisfying a god of some sort and then tapping into the god's resources for answers to life's uncertainty. This perception must not be trivialized, because if one cannot attain to the power of truth—or more appropriately, the power of God—then settling for lesser powers becomes a necessary plan. Man knows how to search for power in God's rival, who answers by sacrificial blood. The quest leaves much to be desired, as it does not answer to the well-being of the soul and abundance of life; it merely responds to and satisfies the request for which the blood was shed, leaving the seeker subject to returning again and again, more like a victim of the ritual than a satisfied customer.

And the Lord spoke to Moses, saying, "Speak to Aaron, to his sons, and to all the children of Israel, and say to them, 'This is the thing which the Lord has commanded, saying: "Whatever man of the house of Israel who kills an ox or lamb or goat in the camp, or who kills it outside the camp, and does not bring it to the door of the tabernacle of meeting to offer an offering to the Lord before the tabernacle of the Lord, the guilt of bloodshed shall be imputed to that man. He has shed blood; and that man shall be cut off from among his people, to the end that the children of Israel may bring their sacrifices which they offer in the open field, that they may bring them to the Lord at the door of the tabernacle of meeting, to the priest, and offer them as peace offerings to the Lord. And the priest shall sprinkle the blood on the altar of the Lord at the door of the tabernacle of meeting, and burn the fat for a sweet aroma to the Lord. They shall no more offer their sacrifices to demons, after whom they have played the harlot. This shall be a statute forever for them throughout their generations." (Leviticus 17:1–7)

Blood for Halloween: I consider Halloween one of the best-kept secrets of a well-told lie. It has penetrated the world by painting a canvas of costumes, candies and a harmless innocence of ghosts, witches, skeletons, coffins, graves and scary scenes. This is a misnomer. How can the remains of death that humans revisit yearly in the ghastliest settings be harmlessly innocent? Those of us whose loved ones have passed on understand the painful emptiness death brings, and feel the need to guard our hearts against sorrow. How, then, can we revisit the frightful portrayal of lives passed on and find it entertaining? What a lie!

Research of the meaning of the name *Halloween* and its history tells of a day to honor dead saints and to protect the Celtics from the dead of the past. History handed down may not be as accurate as it should, but we have a responsibility to engage in profitable and noble celebrations. Can we enjoy the dead by raising their skeletons and coffins to decorate our yards, then add the gloom of cobwebs, witches and lights while little kids roam our streets, begging for candy, and in the meantime being ever careful of possible abduction? Shall we also turn a blind eye to the many animals and pets that go missing at Halloween? Exodus 22:20 says, "He who sacrifices to any god, except to the Lord only, he shall be utterly destroyed."

Blood in bestiality: Exodus 22:19 says, "Whoever lies with an animal shall surely be put to death."

God assured His children through Isaiah, the prophet, that God is fully capable of hearing and saving when they called. But He told them they were separated from Him because of iniquities and sins. God literally hides His face from the violator whose hands are defiled with blood, whose fingers are defiled with iniquity, whose lips speaks lies and whose tongue mutters perverseness.

Defilement through blood speaks a language that is not easily analyzed. It adds a crippling effect to life, and its paralytic symptoms have no rhyme or reason. The only uniformed detectable pattern after we have violated blood's sacredness is misfortune that sticks like glue. God clearly tells us in His Word to stay away from the defilement of blood or He will cast us out from His face and visit the punishment of the iniquity upon the land.

Many have placed their sincere trust in the power of the Almighty God and waited patiently for years, praying and seeking the face of God, only to find their predicament recurring time and again. Take a moment to see if the voice of blood is stronger and more potent than the petition. With blood crying against us, it is no longer God who judges but the power of a spiritual force—the power of the abomination and its defilement—that corrupts us and causes our petition to be vomited out instead of answered.

Mercy is available to those who repent. Repentance is a standard that is solemnly upheld by God. His entire kingdom dwells on repentance. In fact, true repentance leads to righteousness. God has reserved a day of final judgment—not today. Today, if you hear His voice, harden not your heart. Today is the day of salvation. He will hear you, preserve you, and give you as a covenant to the people to restore the earth. Now is the acceptable time; now is the day of salvation.

CHAPTER 11

Jesus' Blood

What about the crucifixion?

As Jesus sat down to the Passover meal with His disciples, He discussed the new testament He was about to establish. What was this covenant meal? Well, it may have been roasted lamb, bread without leaven, herbs and wine. The lamb was slaughtered at the temple, and its blood was given as a sacrifice to the living God. Oh yes, this can be compared with blood sacrifices given today (for example, by the Hindus to their god, Kali).

Imagine the bloodshed associated with this national meal. The Passover and many other religious rituals rely on the use of blood to communicate the message of dependence beyond human ability. However, with Jesus' crucifixion pending, a new ritual of the covenant by blood was soon to be instituted. Jesus would die as the sacrificial lamb and change the ritualistic bloodshed of animals used in the Jewish Passover for those who would accept His sacrifice.

The Bible tells the story of Judas, a disciple of Jesus, who covenanted with the leaders of the synagogue for thirty pieces of silver in exchange for the capture of Jesus. Matthew 26:14–16 says, "Then one of the twelve, called Judas Iscariot, went to the Chief Priests and said, 'What are you willing to give me if I deliver Him to you?' And they counted out to him thirty pieces of silver. So from that time he sought opportunity to betray Him."

The night preceding the crucifixion, Judas lead Roman soldiers to the garden of Gethsemane to arrest Jesus and to bring Him face-to-face with the council of priests and Church leaders who were intolerant of His new doctrine. To proselytize His followers with radical beliefs that broke the traditions laid down by Moses was a crime worthy of death under Jewish law, and Jesus certainly did. For example, He constantly worked on the Sabbath. He and His disciples, when going on their mission on the Sabbath with no preparations for the holy day, got hungry and broke corn from the fields. An impotent man at the sheep market pool, Bethesda, was cured of his infirmity on the Sabbath. To add to the offense, Jesus told him to take up his bed and walk. The man was not supposed to carry his bed on the Sabbath.

The grievance was that Jesus attracted a large following. Influence of that magnitude would change the statute of the God of Abraham, Isaac and Jacob forever. It became imperative that the clergy of the Synagogue, called the Sanhedrin, take a stand and cure the Nation of this professed Messiah before the wrath of God descended on them all. Therefore, the plot to crucify Jesus was justified under the terms of Jewish law.

And the High Priest answered and said to Him, "I put You under oath by the Living God: Tell us if You are the Christ, the Son of God!" Jesus said to him, "It is as you said. Nevertheless, I say to you, hereafter you will see the Son of Man sitting at the right hand of the Power, and coming on the clouds of heaven." Then the High Priest tore his clothes, saying, "He has spoken blasphemy! What further need do we have of witnesses? Look, now you have heard His blasphemy! What do you think?" They answered and said, "He is deserving of death." Then they spat in His face and beat Him; and others struck Him with the palms of their hands, saying, "Prophesy to us, Christ! Who is the one who struck You?" (Matthew 26:63–68)

Digging through a bit of history around Jesus' time, the Jewish nation had survived quite a bit of upheaval after being governed by the Ptolemies and Seleucids. These governments intervened in the religious affairs of the Jews, creating ridicule even to the point of committing abominations. The stage had been set for a people who were capable of governing themselves, living under the harsh and sacrilegious dictates of outsiders, to round up a mob and declare war before you could flip a coin.

We can sympathize on the note that constant rebellion against the government to protect their God-given tradition and religious rites was a necessary task; but to have a Jew himself rise up and thwart the sanctity of the law while attracting an enormous following was treason and worthy of death, without question. I can imagine the High Priest Caiaphas and his council devising the ultimate strategy to make an example of this Jesus, who claimed to be Christ, the Messiah, yet did not take on the oppressive government that kept the Nation exploited. Insurrection to advocate death was the only solution.

An incident related by Josephus is Pilate's use of sacred temple money, or corban, to build an aqueduct into Jerusalem (Wars II 9:4; Ant. XVIII 3:2). When protesters gathered, Pilate sent his soldiers, dressed as civilians, into the crowd. On his signal the soldiers began to beat and kill many (Jewish) protesters. (Doig)

During the time of Jesus in history, the Jews were under Roman rule and did not have the authority to pronounce the death sentence. Official orders had to come from the governor of Judea, Pontius Pilate, or Herod Antipas who ruled over Galilee, which included the village of Nazareth where Jesus grew up. Pilate had to answer to Rome about the affairs of Judea. If Pilate could successfully govern Judea, he would have favor in Caesar's eyes. No small task, as the Jews seemed incapable of relinquishing their sacred standards for dictators like Pilate, with eyes for the glamour of effigies, sculptures of rulers or the standards and ways of the Greeks. Yes, some Jews were swayed by bribery and the likes, but all in all, the nation stood for its principles. All this was tuned and timed precisely into the forecast of the Messiah's life.

Jesus Christ, in the hands of the Sanhedrin, took on the persona of a radical dictator who was finally defeated. To spare cruelty would be equal to sending a signal that another intended Messiah could rise up to lead the nation astray. Nothing was spared to make an example of this man whose given name was Yeshua ben Yosef.

The Sanhedrin lead Yeshua ben Yosef to Pilate's court to ask for his death—death by crucifixion. There was no small stir among the people, because it was necessary for Pilate to see this matter as a possible riot in the making and thereby grant Caiaphas and his leaders their wish. If the wish were not granted and a riot ensued, Pilate would once again have to report on his ability to govern, and since this was not a matter of State but one among the people, it was not hard to consent to their wishes and be over with this mob. Not so easy, for Pilate's wife, apparently a woman he trusted, sent a message to him of a troubling dream she had, in fact, she said she had suffered many things in the dream, and Pilate should have nothing to do with the just man the Jews wanted crucified. "I find no fault in this man," Pilate said. "He teaches heresy against our sacred laws throughout our land from Galilee to this place," the response was fierce. Relief came over Pilate at the name Galilee. "Is He a Galilean?" Pilate asked. This was the answer for which he waited. "This man cannot be tried by this court, He belongs under Herod's jurisdiction. Take Him to Herod for your trial." Patience has a way of solving even the most bewildering trials.

The mob and its religious leaders led Jesus away determined under any circumstance to get the death penalty for this danger to the sacred religion of God handed down by their great leader Moses. It was close to the time of Passover and this business had better not drag on as it would become a pollution of the holy feast to be tending to a prisoner. Plus, who would have the time? They had to put this madness to an end, a verdict was needed immediately, and they would raise hell if it was not granted.

Herod seemed strangely accommodating—more of a welcome to the party than a preparation for trial. As the crowd settled for the trial, Herod faced the man that stirred His Nation with miracles, even raising the dead. *Perhaps this man would perform a supernatural wonder this day, and the gods would even appear right in my very presence—yes, this trial is history in the making. The chief priests and the scribes present a rather decisive case. Really, all they want is death by crucifixion, and that is clear. Now it is this man's turn—rather, it is time for the gods to appear.*

Herod began with his questions for Yeshua; there was no response. Patience, patience—these spiritual sorts have a framework that require patience. On and on went the questions, but Herod grew weary. It did not take long for Herod to realize he was being mocked by this prisoner who absolutely refused to give him even a flicker of response—mockery of his authority and seat of honor! Quickly, the questions changed their tone, and ridicule and scorn began to pour out on this witty man. But how was he going to defend himself; surely he needed to—this crowd would have him dead by nightfall.

"This King of the Jews is not dressed appropriately. Please, bring out a gorgeous robe and array this man like a true king!" At Herod's command, Yeshua was donned in the finest garb, while the soldiers helped to accommodate the sarcasm of honoring the King of the Jews, whom Herod found necessary to send back to Pilate.

Pilate had hoped he had seen the last of this throng. What a stubborn people—their belief in their God and their steadfast obedience to protect His laws took them beyond human comprehension. Torn between truth and politics, Pilate pulled out yet another of his tricks on the disquieted mob. "I have other prisoners who have desecrated your laws. According to your custom, at the time of Passover, a prisoner may be released. All these prisoners have been found guilty under your law; however, I will choose to release this Yeshua ben Yosef and pardon His crimes."

The elders and priests would have no such plea. They incited the mob to fury to get the death penalty for Yeshua. Pilate asked, "What evil has He done?" The heated crowd would not be swayed; crucifixion for Yeshua was the only note they chanted. Pilate called for water. He stood before the people, looked in the face of the just man he would sentence to death, and in an act of symbolic innocence, washed his hands. "I am free of the blood of this just man; see you to it."

Then answered all the people, and said, His blood be on us, and on our children. Then released he Barabbas unto them: and when he had scourged Jesus, he delivered him to be crucified. Then the soldiers of the governor took Jesus into the Praetorium, and gathered unto Him the whole garrison of soldiers. And they stripped Him, and put on Him a scarlet robe. And when they had platted a crown of thorns, they put it upon His head, and a reed in His right hand: and they bowed the knee before Him, and mocked Him, saying, Hail, King of the Jews! And they spit upon Him, and took the reed, and smote Him on the head. And after they had mocked Him, they took the robe off Him, and put His own raiment on Him, and led Him away to crucify Him. And as they came out, they found a man of Cyrene, Simon by name: him they compelled to bear His cross. (Matthew 27:25-32)

The brutality preceding the crucifixion intensified beyond the Praetorium, as told in *Verdict of the Shroud.* Cuts and bruises, gashes where His beard was plucked, puncture wounds and a swollen abdomen that lead to His eventual asphyxiation gave an unsightly picture of human torture. Light contusions to severe punctures with dumbbell-shaped markings from the Roman flagrum whip peppered the entire body. (The flagrum is weighted at its many tips with particles of sharpened bone or lead.) The Roman soldiers were given the honor of scourging Jesus with the flagrum—perhaps while He was bent over a scourging post—and 90 to 120 gashes in His flesh have been counted on the shroud of Turin. Well, a three-pronged whip and forty lashes, as mentioned in the Scriptures, calculate accurately that which has been reported. The severity of the scourging may have hastened Jesus' death and caused internal hemorrhaging in the chest cavity, resulting in a buildup of a bloody mix of serum and blood and the eventual death by suffocation. Piercing the chest cavity, as was done to assure death, released blood and water, as reported in John 19:34.

And when they were come unto a place called Golgotha, that is to say, a place of a skull, they gave Him vinegar to drink mingled with gall: and when He had tasted thereof, He would not drink. And they crucified Him, and parted His garments, casting lots: that it might be fulfilled which was spoken by the prophet, "They parted My garments among them, and upon My vesture did they cast lots." And sitting down they watched Him there; And set up over His head His accusation written, This Is Jesus The King Of The Jews. (Matthew 27:33–36)

The importance of the crucifixion can be summed up in the assurance that the ultimate torture sustained by mankind for the payment of sin will not have to be endured by the whomsoever that chooses to embrace salvation through Jesus Christ. A lamb without sin, blemish, spot or wrinkle, examined by three courts, was offered freely as a sacrifice for those who err at the call. In the beginning, sin entered the world by one man, Adam; therefore, it is justified that by one man, Jesus Christ, there is an offering of righteousness for all.

Man's incompetence to match the wiles of the Devil made it necessary for Christ to confront and destroy the power of evil that ruled the life of man. Through death, Christ entered the domain of hell and stripped the authority that bound man to sin. Who else could have loosed the seal, who else knows the secrets of hell, who else could have been chosen to fight the enemy of God, who else could have offered redemption for man? (Revelation 5)

What has Jehovah God done for His people? He provided an escape from the hordes of hell. Escape by simply accepting the offering of the blood of His Son Jesus, the Christ. Did Christ offer a solution to earthly dictatorship? Yes, He did. He empowered man beyond his physical ability to withstand and defeat the hosts of darkness that swarm the earth with manifestations of evil that thrive on dictators.

And the dictator within—the ever-brewing taste for it all? Where shall I run? For to battle with that which I cannot see is hopelessly futile; the battle that cannot be seen by physical eyes has the capacity to change the heart and spirit of man and shackle him to unimaginative darkness. Yet greater and more baleful than the tyranny and ugliness of worldly or neighborly dictators are the destructive, shameful patterns of our own personal lives we have learned to shove in the closets of life with the hope they will be on their best behavior when we turn on the light. The trouble is, they are true to their designs; shame and destruction waft around their prey like thick clouds of monsters that choke out the sweetness of life—if not for the blood of Jesus Christ.

CHAPTER 12

The Covenant of Marriage

One of the answers to solving life's mystery of success.

The covenant of marriage is designed to be ratified upon the shedding of blood from the unique bond to be shared between a man and his wife. The wife presents a virtuous body to her husband, and a holy covenant is cut and sealed between them in sexual intimacy as man and woman ultimately become one.

The shedding of blood in the covenant of marriage elevates the institution of marriage from a mere earthly agreement to a spiritual knot—the making of two individuals into one. The internal mixing of blood and fluids within the body, designed ingeniously as only our Creator could, creates a bonding exchange as man and wife hold onto each other and the body speaks its own excited language in flames of emotional and physical tones.

This mysterious union bypasses the knowledge of the physical eye and encapsulates the legalities of spirituality, enabling the two with supernatural powers that guarantees a united force to successfully combat and destroy the enemies of the dream of sweet love and harmony envisioned for the life of the marriage.

Virtue however, is the foundation on which this covenant is built. Making this case seems more of an allegation of insult than an absorbable truth. The honor of virtue is no longer a gift reserved for the marriage bed. Society does not wave red flags of warning for impurity.

The rumor mill of gossip for the suspected young girl who seems to be passing out her jewel has dried up. So easy it is for precious virgins to be taken—and not just once, but passed over and handed over as cheaply as candy. The factors that desecrate the institution and cheapen the parties are at the helm of the vessel that destroy marriage. The truth is that impurities introduced before marriage and into marriage create its demise. The demise may begin with husband and wife but spreads its fangs from the children of the union down through generations.

Impurities create dissension, dissension breeds disgust, disgust entertains deceit, deceit is the cohabiting partner of lust, lust is driven by brokenness, and brokenness is the product of impurity. *Like father, like son. Monkey see, monkey do. The apple doesn't fall far from the tree.* These clichés have long existed to prove generational curses are kept alive within families. We call them curses but never stop to explore their beginnings, and if a family member tries to break the mold, somehow it triggers a sense of intolerance. People we love and care for suddenly become the enemy, and from our souls gush distaste strong enough to produce lifelong adversaries.

Who wins? No one. What do we gain? Absolutely nothing! However, the pressure in our souls to carry out this vindication of keeping our adversarial differences alive is rock solid. Instead of watching over and caring for our sisters and cousins, we isolate ourselves and gloat when the byproducts of our indifferences take their toll. You may ask, how can we fight against the passion of our souls to satisfy that which we cannot even fathom? I say, think in terms of the beneficiary. If I benefit, then hand over the blessings—cough it up; bring it. If not, then the truth must be that my passion is controlled, and I am not the master of this game. Someone precious has been burnt by the stigma of my coldness, and somewhere inside, it does affect me; even through layers of "serves her right" is hidden the painful truth that I am not immune, and love can be the only answer.

But let's stay closer to the initial covenant. In a broken home, where vows have been replaced by the cruelty of unkind words and the deceit of malicious actions, the first-line recipients are usually the vulnerable offspring. Here is how it works. The covenant of love is broken, and it invites dark, ugly thoughts that generate revolting behaviors. Consider the fact that these actions are only introduced after a particular incident, and they serve to isolate at least one party of the covenant. Broken covenants remove the covering needed to protect the vulnerable. The weaker ones are exposed to the greater danger, while the stronger are usually rendered insensitive to truth.

Soon the spirit of brokenness invites emptiness, which leads to a search for fulfillment not only for the adults, but also for the children. For example, young girls with absentee fathers spend their entire lifetime searching for fathers to fill the gap; the quest is probed by periods of testing as they pause long enough to find out if 'this catch' is father material. Moving on is not unusual, because each protégée must be like her real father, flaws and all, or he has failed the test. As she moves on, her heart becomes more detached and increasingly angry. Let's not mention the baggage she incurs as the journey progresses; plus, if that journey includes a child, she becomes the ingrained role model for that youngster's life.

Young boys from broken homes find comfort in roaming and filling time with intriguingly creative mischief. Interestingly, a man never seems comfortable in staying where chaos exists unless he is the author of it. Another amazing observation is that young boys find comfort in numbers, and instinctively, a leader emerges—a leader who takes the group to the edge and earns the sought-after respect men give to trailblazers. Excitement builds, and brotherhood is born. Ripping him from the hood is like taking another family member from his life, and because these members intrigue his fantasy, wives who eventually find the ticket to his heart—or like I say, are admitted to the club—are married to his shadow. His interest in the marriage is divided between his ability to keep the chase of his fresh conquest alive (that is, how stimulating can this marriage be) versus the edge experienced when his freedom was still intact. A wife given the task of holding him back from the boys becomes a magician in her own rights.

Wives of broken marriages experience the gut-wrenching spirit of disillusionment that results in bitterness. Even if the woman produced the folly that created the downward spiral of the relationship, she continuously questions the sincerity of the husband who did not understand her vulnerability and sees his lack of comprehension as a betrayal rather than a lack of wisdom. As a mother, she is not careful to watch over her daughter and guide her diligently out of the path of predators who seek to reduce her to a notch in the belt and the gratification of a demented mind. Or, as she becomes absorbed in her torturous misfortune, the signs and cries for attention from her daughter are misinterpreted and blend with her sorrows as part of the package of failure. For her son, it becomes a welcome solution that he finds comfort elsewhere, as her bosom of love is sapped. For her husband, she builds contempt and connives lessons which she hopes will drive him to his knees before her lordship so that she can declare herself successful in the business of conquering her man.

It is the glory of men to stand tall, and in order to stand tall, he must believe he is free—truly free. A man who is under the thumb of his bride will release his body from the grip yet leave his ghost so she will believe she is still in charge. Husbands hide pain and unfulfillment in crafts that make them feel powerful. In this marriage, his created portal to shine is destroyed, and the joy of recreating the castle is stolen. But true to his manly nature, he will rise again—especially in the public's eye. Power to rise is derived from the strangest of modes. Power could be the merciless blows he is propelled to administer when he feels the collapse of his world; power could be the next world empire that rises from rubbish; power could be drugs, alcohol and the like, true to the old, old tale that they numb the pain.

The beneficiaries of destroyed marriage vows are not the family members. That which enjoys this trip has got to be the spirit of brokenness or the spirits of impurity. Too many subtle unpleasantries that rob the love and joy of family are introduced to make a broken marriage a mere intolerance of behavior or irreconcilable differences. Division, not separation, is enough ground for contrary spirits to thrive. Father tearing in one direction, mother tugging in another, kids running wild, wolves stealing precious lives. We have to see that in it all, there are spirits—spirits of lust, spirits of jealousy, spirits of theft, spirits of deceit, spirits of torment, spirits of maliciousness, spirits of greed, sickness, death... and the list goes on. It does not take a stretch of the imagination to realize that unwanted intrusions lead to immorality, which leaves scarred instead of virtuous women and men for future generations.

But quietly, very quietly, someone or something is cashing in on it all. Take off your shoes—*shhh.* Please, on your tippy toes, follow me. Let's go to the attic; I want to show you something. Close your eyes; now open them. Look! See the smoke of intoxication oozing from the pipes of death? Smell the putrid air of sulfur mixed with the foul smell of decay, the smell of rotting flesh. Look around at your feet; see the wet and clammy crawling creatures like miniature worms? Now, let your eyes focus through the thick blackness. Can you see the oversized, black, venomous creatures at the table, enjoying this party? This is their home now; they rule from here.

It would be advantageous if we could step beyond the natural into the world that controls mankind. How advantageous? I really do not know, because man's nature is to create immunity to that which is familiar. But what if we could actually see the spirits at work in our loved ones—would we fight for them? Naturally, we see the drunken stupor of husbands or wives as they yield themselves over to rage and vile outbursts that send shock waves throughout the house and frighten everyone into subjection. At times, we feel sickness overwhelm our bodies, taking its toll especially on our ability to make conscious decisions—too weak to concentrate—the brain feels like it has turned to mush.

But perhaps the most deadly fuel that feeds the foreboding spirits are the words of death we speak. Curse words are the spiritual language of hell. They have the power to call up slime of the darkest order and set it to work in our lives. Have you ever noticed that profanity has a different meaning in every given context? That's the language of the spirits of hell, and we empower the hordes of death every time we sound off.

Some of the grossest sins we commit are done in the privacy of our homes. Surely, a man's home is his temple. There we offer up the sacrifices of our lips. We bring to it the fruits of our labor. We decorate as lavishly or as carelessly as we choose, and it becomes the resting place of many of our earthly treasures. We are our true selves at home; there are no cover-ups, our guards are down and our imaginations are unleashed. Outside the home, we portray the image we want the public to perceive. Of course, there is the exceptional unraveling that opens up truth, but home is reality. Let's face it; when our homes are not sanctified, our lives are chaotic. When the sanctification of the blood of the Lord Jesus Christ is completed in our homes, God will execute a mighty deliverance.

Love—not tolerance or fear, but true love—can save any marriage. Love takes the fight into the chamber of God and implores His hand for mercy. Love brings back the gift of mercy and washes the house of the filth and muck that has begun to grow. Love goes back to the chamber of God and implores His hand for grace. Grace is used to refurbish and decorate. Again, love travels to the portals of heaven, but this time, it enters the courts of truth; it stays a while as a case is made. This time, the petition is more demanding; it wants the presence of the Most High.

To return with the Spirit of God necessitates an entourage of angels bearing the Word of truth, righteousness, peace and forgiveness to mend and put hearts back together. This is no small task. To get into courts of the Almighty, there must be thanksgiving and worship; the return trip is expected to meet with great opposition. The attic has been cleaned out, but the spirits are lurking, waiting for an opportunity to return. If they see heavenly reinforcement, there will be an all-out war.

A decision is made. Love will go back and mount a defense of prayer for seven days, during which time different angels will be dispatched to bring the request bit by bit. Truth will be the first to come in tiny doses; forgiveness will follow. Forgiveness is hated by the spirits of darkness, and they seem to detect it from miles away. Love has to carefully watch for it and vow to help protect its safe arrival. If only we could see life as it truly is.

The ability to regain the wholesomeness and beauty in marriage rests on forgiveness and truth. Husband and wife become vulnerable and open without anger and without bitterness. Truth symbolizes the purifier and forgiveness the ointment for healing. The next step, of course, is reinstatement of the covenant. This time, the covenant is cut and solidified with the blood of the Lord Jesus Christ, the third party and keeper of the covenant of marriage.

Restoration of the covenant comes through cleansing. As intended by God, this exclusive bond, shared by man and wife, is similar to the covenant Christ made with the Church. Christ entered into a covenant with His bride, the Church, by laying down His life for the Church so He might sanctify and cleanse it. (Ephesians 5:23–30) Really, Christ made provision to keep the Church as a pure and undefiled possession. Why? Impurities break covenants. Once undesirables, foreign matters, not-part-of-the-covenant particles enter the marriage, it begins to fall apart. Therefore, there remains a perpetual source of cleansing for the bride of Christ so that she would not fall prey to the traps that beget impurity.

Covenants are symbolic of protection. God told Israel to eat the Passover in their houses—the houses where the lambs were kept—signifying that the house where the lamb is and where the blood of the lamb was shed and placed on the doorposts and lintel was sanctified as a tabernacle, a holy place, because the Lord commanded it so. Here lies the instruction to purify and sanctify our homes. This is the answer to driving out the works of unrighteousness from our dwelling places and making them holy unto the Lord.

CHAPTER 13

Dabbling

> Blessed be the name of God forever and ever; wisdom and might are His and He changes times and seasons. —Daniel 2:20–21

This business of life has mesmerized us all. A woman is pregnant. A baby is being formed and shaped in the womb, and without fail, we know what to expect at the time of birth. "Boy or girl?" Crossed species cannot make it to term, because the mixing of genomic material creates intolerance by the carrier's immune system, and abortion is automatic. Therefore, a kangaroo cannot give birth to a fly, and humans cannot give birth to whales.

You may ask, where on earth is this idea going? Well, let's take this notion a little further. In the religions of the world, theories abound. Every religion states its history and origin with stories of earthly gods and spiritual contacts (more or less). The universal train of thought is that religion offers hope and answers to the unfathomable pursuits of the earth and gives comfort regarding the spiritual unknown (and certainly an eternal or continual factor). How can one accurately decipher the truth in it all? The best answer the mind can conceive is to combine the lot and then rest in the assurance that somewhere in it all lays the answer. However, the combination conflicts, and reassurance fails instead of producing satisfaction, resulting in the need for choice. What parts or doctrines of religion need the systemic abortion, so wonderfully given by the natural immunity of the body, so that man may be led to the purity of the true and living God?

It rings in the subconscious: *Easy, the answers have got to be easy; just feels like I am missing a basic, simple truth.* This indispensable requirement tugs at the soul of man and laments, calling for our attention—sometimes even more than our basic necessities, especially when someone around us dies.

Death becomes a cruel reminder of how unsteady this tightrope walk of life truly is. The soul mourns and brings a wave of sadness that is shared in common grief. The heart is weakened, and barriers that have withstood many moons lower themselves without prejudice or scorn. Death seems to laugh in the face of uncertainty with mockery and insults that become unbearable, and we cry out with agony—perhaps more so out of our insecurity than for the soul of the departed.

It is in the face of this insecurity that man has conjured what I wish to call the god-complex. The searching of the soul for the escape from death has lead us through a maze of answers to which we grasp for consolation. Astrology has paved the path for spells, hexes and magic. Dabbling in these crafts has opened the doors to otherworldly experiences that bring a daring hope of conquering the unknown. The invitation to explore and go beyond takes the soul to new heights as it brings the enchanter to levels that grant empowerment beyond natural abilities. Solutions are exchanged at costs as astronomical as the illusions presented, and a hush is breathed over the process, because we know this kind of tampering is taboo. Consequently, the mind pushes the limits of acceptance and belief, as this kind of dabbling seems to be the only answer.

The stakes in this gamble then become the degree to which I believe, and we are warned that this dabbling works on belief. Without belief, it will not work. Appropriately, the responsibility of success is removed from the enchanter, as in the recesses of our souls, we know that the limitations are countlessly infinite. Disturbing truths of this danger zone that boggle the mind are laid unsettlingly to rest, and a new assertion is bought (not only with cash, but bought in the mind) as we tell ourselves, *This will work.* Hail to the day that the requests become granted, for this was all that was needed to unboggle the mind. But then reality strikes, and strikes with ruthless absolutes, when death, like a loathsome dragon, rears its ugly head and deals its fatal blow.

Dreams, premonitions and an atmosphere of the uncertainty of life also cast their toll on the mind. Do dreams really hold the key to unlocking answers of the future? Yes, they do! In Matthew 2, the angel of the Lord appeared to Joseph through a dream and told him to take his young child and wife and flee to the safety of Egypt, as the child was in danger of being killed.

What about disastrous dreams? Let's probe this concept. Sleep is the uncontrolled state the body enters—a sort of death-like phenomenon. It is in this state of abandonment of the will and its desires that dreams are produced. This means that dreams come to us from a means beyond human comprehension, and to complicate matters, they sometimes come true. I have discovered that to remember a dream is to control the future. How? This depends on the god you serve. Is your god able to cancel the effects of that which you have envisioned if you ask in prayer? Does your god use dreams to forewarn you of the plans of darkness against your life, thereby empowering you to abort the activity at the gates of destruction? Does your god care enough that his guiding hand covers and protects you even in your dreams?

Daniel answered in the presence of the king, and said, The secret which the king hath demanded cannot the wise men, the astrologers, the magicians, the soothsayers, show unto the king; But there is a God in heaven that reveals secrets, and makes known to the king Nebuchadnezzar what shall be in the latter days. The dream and the visions of your head upon your bed are these; as for you, O king, your thoughts came into your mind upon your bed, what should come to pass hereafter: and He that reveals secrets makes known to you what shall come to pass. (Daniel 2:27–29)

Yes, it is true that practice becomes perfect; the more I dabble, the better I become. Irresistible enticements bestow empowerment on their seekers when through weakness of the mind comes surrender to their indulgence. My life is the sum of my thoughts and actions. I will never be intrigued by that which I cannot perceive. I will never be driven to fulfill dreams that my mind cannot plan. The achievements of my life tell the story of my passion, and as I yield, they are perfected, taking me to spheres of happiness. Matthew 6:32–33 says, "For your heavenly Father knows that ye have need of all these things. But seek ye first the kingdom of God, and His righteousness; and all these things shall be added unto you." It is amazing that in just one book, so many answers can be found; and yes, man must tap into the spiritual realm, or his soul will never be satisfied or accomplished.

No author has walked away and chosen not to be identified with the greatness of a published work. No farmer has seen his crops ready for harvest and then abandoned his hard labor and left them to die. No designer being praised for the uniqueness of a new concept denies his work. It is not possible that the Creator would deny access to the created, for God designed man that they both would fellowship together. God is recruiting worshipers, and the only requirement is that they worship Him in Spirit and in truth. God will never turn away from those who seek Him with their whole heart.

The offer is extended that you dabble with the Holy Spirit—better known as the Presence of God. Start with truth—an acknowledgment of who you are and where you have been. Align yourself with the holiness of God, and invite your Creator to touch your life again.

Become intrigued by the fellowship and enticed by the possibilities of the Almighty so that it becomes a weakness—a passion. Sit at the feet of love, and let God's beauty unravel.

CHAPTER 14

The Role of the Holy Spirit

For as many as are led by the Spirit of God, these are sons of God. —Romans 8:14

Among all the important things that Jesus Christ came to fulfill is a gift that cannot be ignored—the giving of the Holy Spirit. It would be unjust to end this book without acknowledging and thanking the Holy Spirit for the revelation of the work of the Lord Jesus Christ. As individual as we all are, so are our opinions. As we study the Bible or search for the truth, and revelation of the Father God through His Son, the Lord Jesus Christ, man generates absurdities, lies, fables, rhetoric, and even brand new doctrines. However, those who have diligently searched for the Father through His Son, Jesus Christ, being led by the Holy Spirit, have been successful in fulfilling their God-given destiny and unleashing mysteries from the heart of the Father.

Jesus responded to Peter's answer, "Flesh and blood did not reveal this to you, but my Father which is in Heaven," and upon this revelation—upon the seeking of the truth of God, upon those who pursue the heart of God—"I will build my Church and the gates of hell shall not prevail. And I will give to you the keys of the Kingdom of Heaven, and whatsoever you bind on earth will be bound in heaven, and whatsoever you loose on earth will be loosed in heaven." (Matthew 16:13–19)

Why keys to the kingdom of heaven? It is the seat or the gate of earthly activity. It all begins first in the spirit. To grasp this concept, we first need to be introduced into the world called the heavenlies and then learn to live in it. Followers of Christ are given the gift of the Presence of God to usher them in and navigate its realms.

In Paul's first letter to the Corinthians, he engaged them in a mystery. Those who have found Christ the Lord speak the wisdom of God with words that seem like foolishness. This incomprehensible theory has also been hidden from the rulers of this age—the rulers who became blinded into crucifying the Lord of Glory. God ordained this hidden wisdom for the glory of those who choose to follow His lead, and reveals it to them by His Spirit: for the Spirit searches all things, yes, the deep things of God.

The Presence of the Lord that dwells in the heart of the believer searches the deep truths of God and reveals them to the heart and understanding of that man. As Paul said, no one knows the heart of another man; only an individual can claim to truly know who he or she is. So it is with Christ; just acknowledging God does not make us privy to the Spirit of God. The relationship has to be real; the fellowship has to become intimate. The heart has to be invested, and then God grants His Presence so that we may know Him. This is not done in our own understanding, but we know Him by His Spirit—the uniting of God and man. That knowledge produces the wisdom and teaching on the inside, conducted by the Holy Spirit of God; it compares spiritual things with spiritual things. There is a free flow of the knowledge and wisdom God possesses, and it confuses the minds of those who have no access to its depth. Not until it is displayed in the earth and produces a never-before-experienced phenomenon can others perceive the depth of the experience that came from the Spirit of God on the inside of those chosen to bring God to the earth through His Spirit. Yes, some people do have the mind of Christ.

All things are of God, are made by God, and serve the purposes of God. Therefore, the Holy Spirit takes us through the spiritual realm on a discovery of the vastness of God. Some theologians may disagree and make the point that the Holy Spirit was the promise of the Father given for the saints to live here on earth. However, if we are born again of the Spirit and not of the flesh, then our journey is spiritual, not earthly. Our guide must be through the realms of the spirit in order to successfully maneuver the facets of earth.

In Ephesians 4, Paul wrote that when Christ ascended, He gave gifts to men measured by the yardstick of grace. These spiritual gifts were to unify the body of Christ in the faith and bring us to the knowledge of the Son of God, and among other things, help us uncover the infinity of the stature of Christ.

In 1 Corinthians 12, the writings explain how the Holy Spirit perfects those who desire to be holy. It starts by telling us we would revert to dumb idols in the ignorance of our minds as a type of substitute or the next best thing to tapping into the spirit world through the leading of Christ. Then it goes on to say that the Holy Spirit distributes gifts that are manifested in varying forms and for all kinds of situations which are given to the saints for their profit, ultimately, that we can attain to the stature and holiness of Christ.

Let's explore God's gift of miracles, prophecy, and tongues. Miracles are expressions of the spirit realm seen on earth by physical eyes; miracles are a supernatural display for human benefit. Prophecy is not a wish list coming to pass by mere speech. Prophecy is the heart of man tapped into the heart of God; the future is communicated and man voices the knowledge of God on the earth.

Tongues are most interesting. Many Christians have placed this gift on the back burner, and some have hoped it would disintegrate. It has been ridiculed, contradicted, dubbed a foolishness of the mind, and more. However, tongues are simply the language of God. We speak the language of our native tongue, and a stranger is awed by its fluency and someone else's understanding of it. So it is, the man that navigates the spiritual realm through the Holy Spirit speaks the language of God fluently, and does not seek its understanding for physical accountability, because really, the communication was not for physical understanding but rather for the physical manifestation of the will of God spoken in the earth.

Take a ride with me through the heavenlies. Angels of God are ushering us through the realms of the spirit. (Remember, we are seated in heavenly places in Christ Jesus.) The Holy Spirit or the Presence of God is our guide, and as we see and experience new dimensions, we become awed by the splendor and glory of it all. Then, in heavenly language, we begin to adore the awesomeness of our Father God, and the native language of heaven rolls off our tongues. Worship flows to the Most High, who was, and is, and is to come.

It is not hard to imagine that love is intricately tied to spiritual gifts. When we have experienced God in His majestic glory, the trivialities of life lose their impact on our souls; the grip and struggle of sin wane in the light of the experience of God's holy Presence. First Corinthians 13 says that love never fails, because I have been perfected with just a glimpse of the magnificence of love, and there is no failure in God. Lost in the beauty of God's grace, captured by the sweetness of His voice and mesmerized by the tenderness of the moment, my earthly achievements pale, words fail, and homage is reduced to "Holy, holy, holy; the Lord our God is holy."

CHAPTER 15

The Covenant Communion Passover

This is the day of my new beginning!

The Lord God instituted an ordinance for His people, Israel, to forever destroy the lifelong yoke that stifled them as a nation. So powerful was the ordinance, it became known as the Exodus; and yes, the ordinance was signed in blood. Every family had its own personal experience with the shedding of the blood of a lamb without blemish; then the blood was slathered on the doors and lintel of their homes. Blood was the sign of protection each family proudly displayed at the obedience of God's word. That night, the angel of death would pass through town, and when he saw the blood, he would not enter that house.

In every house without blood, the firstborn was taken. The ache of death was heard far and wide as sorrow was poured out on those without the covering of blood. That which became a great deliverance for the weak was a double-edged sword for the strong. Therefore, it was not difficult for the protected to remember yearly the impact and significance of the passing over of death. This must have been a sacred celebration, with each person recounting an exclusive yet similar story—how by the Word of God and obedience, they were spared.

Years later, Jesus Christ, the Son of God, came to earth and fulfilled the prophecy of this significant ordinance called Passover when He became the eternal Passover lamb. Man was yearning for an answer to the overwhelming disease of sin that plagued the world, so Jesus knew that to become the Christ—the Savior who redeems from sin—He had to offer pure blood, untainted by sin, free from the guile that man was subject to, as only purity could destroy sin. Jesus Christ understood the authority of blood to activate changes spiritually, and He offered Himself willingly to become the payment needed to purchase souls from hell. He was humanity's only hope—the purity of a life not contaminated with sin. Full of compassion for His Father's children and with full knowledge of His Father's request, He accomplished the redemption of man.

As Jesus commemorated the last Passover with His disciples, He laid down a commandment: "Do this in remembrance of me." Interpreted, "Continue to honor the Passover by remembering what I am about to accomplish for you. The blood of goats, lambs, and bulls will cease to be, as they were limited in taking away sins. Now you can enter boldly into the Holy of Holies—not of the earthly tabernacle, but of the heavenly—to converse with God Himself because of my shed blood. Once and for all I am giving myself to the whomsoever at their will. I have consecrated a pathway for you to walk. It will take you to my Father; it will take you home."

What did Jesus Christ accomplish by being our Passover lamb? He purchased man from the curse of sin, the law of sin—restoration of the spirit of man was made. He gave us the privilege to come into the presence of God without a mediator; freedom to enjoy fellowship and audience with a holy God; opportunity to have life and life more abundantly—that is, life to its fullest without skeletons in the closet; life everlasting after death—not reincarnation and its uncertainties, but a life without sorrow, sadness or death, with the presence of a holy God.

Until the spirit that is estranged from God is reconciled, life is only a frustrated, tormented bundle of bondage in the earth. How is this possible? How do I gain access to the only blood that brings life? Jesus explained this mystery in St. John 6. Jesus was sent from heaven to become the broken sacrifice for all people—broken by beatings and the wounding of His body plus being offered in death by crucifixion—and then given as a free will offering to the Father God.

When Jesus entered heaven and handed His blood to His Father as the completed task He was sent to earth to accomplish, He said, "Whoso eats my flesh and drinks my blood has eternal life." (St. John 6:54) He went on to explain that anyone who eats of His flesh and drinks of His blood lives in Him, the Christ, and He in turn lives in that man. There is more. Jesus explained that He lives in His Father God, so those who partake of Him will become part of the spiritual union and the greatness that is unique to the character of Christ.

The plan God gave to gather His children back to Him after the fall of Adam in no way has to appeal to or make sense to the minds of humans. God does not predicate His kingdom on man's approval. All He requires is faith. To trust in the Lord with all our hearts and not to trust with our understanding is the key to unlocking the mysteries of the Spirit, as any other spiritual guide will lead to damnation.

It seems necessary to search out this puzzle and place the pieces in their perspective arrangement in order to effect a conclusion that satisfies the soul. I agree—but that is the solution we apply in the absence of trust. Trust is blind, not dumb. It would be foolish to trust in that which has not been proven. It is senseless to roll over for that which has previously failed. Jesus Christ has never failed. All that He set out to accomplish has been effectively accomplished surpassing human imagination; why would He fail now?

Jesus said, "He that eats of this bread will live forever." (St. John 6:51) Perhaps the greatest desire of the human heart is to live forever. In some way or perhaps in some form, we want to continue life. However, the life that Christ offers is not as some of us wish. If only we could catch a glimpse of the beauty of forever with Christ; then we would rise in dimensions of sacred purity to measure up to the riches of that inheritance. When we partake of the body and the blood of Christ, we become as He is and transition from this life into the wealth of the treasure that awaits those who are found in Him.

Is this just a wonderful theory? Many have believed, trusted, rolled over, yielded and extended blind faith, and no such treasure has been found. Again, this revelation is not based on the life of another; this is a truth that you (and only you) must steadfastly find. Again, this is not a proven concept that catches on like wildfire that men throng to taste of because, *it worked for my next-door neighbor*. This is the ultimate personal experience for your life as you are found in Christ. God is not on the sales pitch of the century, working tirelessly to gain customers so His kingdom can be proven to be legitimate. Instead, He is sweetly beckoning to you to come to His fountain of life.

"The Words I speak unto you are Spirit and life." (St. John 6:63) This is my favorite line in the Bible. I am humbled to be chosen for the life of Christ to be deposited in me. I await the spiritual awakening that takes place daily as I submit myself to the Spirit of God. My belief no longer rests in the epiphany or euphoria of the moment my desires become reality, but it rests in my God. His decisions are wiser and more perfect than my vision; His gift of life is more real than this moment in time. His Presence and heart that beats within me are more absolute than my eyes can fathom. Life becomes a bundle of uncertainty filled with exciting wonder as He unfolds His will in me by His Spirit, which I have allowed to dwell in me by faith.

To partake of the body and blood of the Lord Jesus Christ, then, is the outward obedience to the living promise contained in my body. I have accepted Jesus Christ as Lord and Savior, not as fire insurance (that I may be spared from the pangs of hell's fire), not as a guarantor of earthly wealth, not because I have been handed this concept of religion by my parents. Indeed, I have accepted the truth that God has revealed Himself to me, for that which He has taken a hold of me for.

With full consciousness that my requests are made to the only true God through His Son, the Lord Jesus Christ, I bless the bread and the wine—just as in the Passover meal—and offer it up to God to become the body and blood of His Son, the Lord Jesus Christ. I partake joyfully by faith, knowing that I do show forth the Lord's death till He comes. In Matthew's account of Jesus' last Passover with His disciples, Jesus took bread and a cup, blessed them, and gave thanks to the Father. He then gave them to His disciples and told them, "This is My body, this is My blood, a new testament for the remission of sins." (Matthew 26:28)

To partake of the Lord's body and blood in this holy communion is to erase abominations and the violations of blood—to wipe out destructive ordinances that have taken effect because of my sins, transgressions, and iniquity. Partaking of this new covenant lays a new path to my life. It releases me from the debts of darkness, promises to fulfill that which I cannot pay, and the blood required at my hand for my involvement in sin. As I join with the ranks of holy men and women who dedicate themselves to serving the kingdom of the Lord Jesus Christ, I lay my signature in blood—the blood of Christ—through holy communion.

It is painted in the realms of the heavenlies that I now belong to the company of Christ's Saints. Therefore, I embody the Christ-minded truth and become a slave to the Spirit of the living God so that I may know Him in the power of a resurrected Lord. Through His conquest of hell and death, I am empowered to be free of the grip of destructive forces and their effect on my mind and body. I will know Him in the fellowship of His sufferings, not thinking it robbery to be equal with God but yielding my body to be buffeted until it is perfected. When the enemy has lost his strength of torment, pain, and temptation, I will rise in Christ over that which subjects man to evil. Then coming into harmony with Christ's death, I rise to take ground that only the undefeated by the sting of death can conquer.

The Passover has its origin in the lives of the Israelites, who cried out to God for deliverance. God instituted the Passover four days before a mighty deliverance. God's instructions were that every household take a lamb and keep it in the home for four days. When those days were ended, they were to kill the lambs and spread the blood over the doors and lintel of the houses.

In the Covenant Communion Passover, we will spend four days with the Lamb of God, Jesus Christ, through the Holy Spirit, by completing the following instructions.

Let's partake of the covenant of the blood of the Lord Jesus Christ.

Step 1—Repent of Your Sins by Saying This Prayer:

God of Abraham, Isaac and Jacob, you who sent your Son, Jesus Christ, to die for my sins, I confess this day that I have sinned and come short of the glory of God. I have done evil in your sight, but with the understanding and knowledge of your love, I bow in repentance before you. Please take away my sins, and wash me in the blood of the Lord Jesus Christ; purge me, and make me clean. I believe in my heart that you hear me, and despite my many wrongs and failures, you now forgive me because of your grace and love. I humbly accept your forgiveness, and I forgive those who have wronged and hurt me. I ask you this day for a new beginning; I ask that you will send angels to minister to me. I ask that you will send your Holy Spirit to guide me and lead me into all truth. I believe that upon confessing my sins and asking you to come and live in my heart, you will, and my life will begin anew as I listen to hear your voice and yield in obedience to it. Amen.

Step 2—Ask for the Holy Spirit's Guidance with this Prayer:

Dear Jesus Christ, Son of the living God, you made a promise to your disciples when you were on earth that they would receive power when the Holy Spirit came upon them. I ask now for the power to become a son of the Most High God. I realize that the Holy Spirit is my spiritual guardian as I enter this new life with you. I ask that you will fill me with the Holy Spirit so that I may become holy as you, oh Lord God, are holy. Amen.

Step 3—Take the Cup that Is Made of Wine or Any Fruit of the Vine and Bread, and Bless Them by Saying this Prayer:

Father God, I thank you that you hear me. I present this cup to you, and by faith, I ask that you bless it to become the blood of the Lord Jesus Christ. I bless the bread also, in the name of Jesus Christ, to become the broken body of Jesus Christ, my Lord and Savior. I partake of these in faith, believing in and remembering the Lord's death and His blood that was poured out for my life so that I may become whole. As I partake, dear Lord, enrich my life with your presence and glory, and let your favor shine upon me. Lead me in the paths of righteousness for your name's sake, sanctify and make me clean, and let me be an instrument for the glory of God. Eradicate the plans of hell against me, deliver me from evil, and lead me not into temptation. Walk with me, and instruct me in your way, because I trust you. Amen.

Step 4—Day 1—Morning

Take the cup and the bread to the altar you have prepared for this sacred time.

Read Exodus 12:1–7 and Luke 22:14–32.

Meditation: Make this a time of thankfulness to God for the provision of His Son, the Lord Jesus Christ, and the plan of salvation. Reflect on the gift of God's Son and His crucifixion that provided the shed blood needed to purchase us from the ravishes of sin.

Pray: My Father God, thank You for sending your Son, Jesus Christ, to die shamefully for me so that I may obtain pardon for my sins. Thank you for opening my ears to hear and my heart to believe your Word. I receive by faith this truth of salvation and pledge to surrender the rest of my life to your trust and care. Amen.
Pray the Lord's blessing upon the cup and the bread, and then eat and drink all of it.

Day 1—Noon

Take the cup and the bread to the altar you have prepared for this sacred time.

Read Exodus 12:8–14 and Matthew 16:13–27.

Meditation: Ask the Lord to speak to you so that you will hear and know His voice. In return, He asks that you deny yourself the habits of the past that are contrary to His holiness. Reflect on the habits and actions of the past, and renounce them.

Pray: Heavenly Father, I have accepted your sacrifice for my life that was given through Jesus Christ. As I reflect on my past, I ask for a complete washing and cleansing from every involvement in every sin that I have yielded my mind, soul, and body to. I let go, forsake, renounce, cancel, and abandon the deeds and involvement of the past in exchange for the protection, grace, favor and blood of the Lord Jesus Christ. I will rid my mind, possessions and life of any trace of evil, because I am committed to the righteousness and cause of Christ. Amen.

Pray the Lord's blessing upon the cup and the bread, and then eat and drink all of it.

Day 1—Evening

Take the cup and the bread to the altar you have prepared for this sacred time.

Read Exodus 12:15–20 and Mark 8:27-38.

Meditation: A new life requires new action. What can you do to please the Lord? How can you make a difference that will effect changes and cause Christ's life to become a blessing to others?

Pray: Dear Lord, now that I belong to you, will you show me how to please you? I desire to be a blessing in the kingdom of the Lord Jesus Christ. Please take my family under your care, and reveal to them the truth you have revealed to me. Spread your wings of love over us, and speak the blessings of your Word into our lives. Cause us to experience the presence of the Almighty God and desire you in every aspect of our lives. Amen.

Pray the Lord's blessing upon the cup and the bread, and then eat and drink all of it.

Day 2—Morning

Take the cup and the bread to the altar you have prepared for this sacred time.

Read Exodus 12:21–28 and Luke 11:1–36.

Meditation: Blessings will come alive just by asking, seeking, and knocking. You must study and search out the extent of the blessings and favor of God. It is by wisdom, knowledge, and understanding that you will prosper.

Pray: Holy Father, I have abandoned myself to your care, being vulnerable and totally dependent on the Holy Spirit to lead me. However, Lord, it is clear that my surrender must be nurtured by my study and knowledge of who you are. Lead me into truth as I begin my quest for the vastness and completeness of your holiness. I will be your testimony to the world of a life well pleasing to the Almighty and Most High God. Amen.

Pray the Lord's blessing upon the cup and the bread, and then eat and drink all of it.

Day 2—Noon

Take the cup and the bread to the altar you have prepared for this sacred time.

Read Exodus 12:29–36 and John 3:1–21.

Meditation: You are born again as a spiritual man because of the covenant of love God has given you. Sit at the feet of love, pledge your dedication and enjoy this blessing. Because you believe in God and His Son, Jesus Christ, you are not condemned by your past, and your past has no more control over you.

Pray: My Lord and my God, I am truly yours, and you have accepted me into your kingdom as your child because of your great love. I empty my heart and mind of any residue of guilt from the past, because you have forgiven me and freed me of the past. I accept this gift of life and will increase my worship of you, my Father and Lord, in honor of your great love. Amen.

Pray the Lord's blessing upon the cup and the bread, and then eat and drink all of it.

Day 2—Evening

Take the cup and the bread to the altar you have prepared for this sacred time.

Read Exodus 12:37–42 and John 15:1–17.

Meditation: The kingdom of God has its foundation in love. As you learn about God, you must embrace this unconditional love for all people. All your life, God has been there, watching over and caring for you, even when you ignored Him.

Pray: Oh Lord, teach me to love; give me a heart of love just like yours. Remove the thoughts of impurities that present themselves to my mind that I may be like you. I will keep your commandments. I pray for the Spirit of Truth, the Comforter, the Holy Spirit to fill me up with the goodness and love of the Father God. Let your love overwhelm me so that I may naturally pass it on to those around me. Amen.

Pray the Lord's blessing upon the cup and the bread, and then eat and drink all of it.

Day 3—Morning

Take the cup and the bread to the altar you have prepared for this sacred time.

Read Exodus 12:43–51 and Romans 8:1–30.

Meditation: You owe your fleshly desires nothing; you do not have to satisfy your desires! You must tap into the riches and glory of this new life in Christ. You cannot allow circumstances to dictate your actions. Instead, you must crucify the expectations of your head and sacrifice them for the excellence of the knowledge of Christ.

Pray: Abba Father, who art in heaven, holy is your Name. Your kingdom come; your will be done on earth—in my life—as it is in heaven. Give us this day our daily bread, and forgive us our debts as we forgive those who trespass against us. Lead us not into temptation, but deliver us from evil, for yours is the kingdom, the power, and the glory, forever and ever. Amen.

Pray the Lord's blessing upon the cup and the bread, and then eat and drink all of it.

Day 3—Noon

Take the cup and the bread to the altar you have prepared for this sacred time.

Read Genesis 22:1–19 and 1 Peter 1:3–10.

Meditation: The genuineness of your faith will be placed in the fire of God. Greatness is attained through perseverance in that which you believe. Believe in God, His Son the Lord Jesus Christ, and the presence of the Lord, the Holy Spirit. You must persevere and be proven as pure gold.

Pray: Heavenly Father, show me how to be strong in the Lord and in the power of His might. I cover my mind with the truth of the Word of God and ask the Holy Spirit to minister the light of God to my soul so that I will not yield to or become a victim of evil. Let not evil triumph over me, but let the greatness of God be my victory and my life a living sacrifice to God, holy and acceptable, for this is my reasonable service. Amen.

Pray the Lord's blessing upon the cup and the bread, and then eat and drink all of it.

Day 3—Evening

Take the cup and the bread to the altar you have prepared for this sacred time.

Read 2 Chronicles 1:1–17 and Matthew 22:37–40.

Meditation: You are loved by God, and you must reciprocate that love. In this love is all that you need. To honor God is to truly love Him in word and deed. God will not withhold any good thing from you as you walk in holiness before Him.

Pray: Father God, I am ready to explore the wonder and greatness for which you have purposed my life. As I trust you, I believe with all my heart that you will honor me. Like Solomon, I ask for wisdom, knowledge, and understanding so that I may inherit the full extent of the miracles you have for me. Keep me focused on the reality of your truth, and let the foolishness of sin fall beneath my feet. Amen.

Pray the Lord's blessing upon the cup and the bread, and then eat and drink all of it.

Day 4—Morning

Take the cup and the bread to the altar you have prepared for this sacred time.

Read Matthew 8:1–13 and John 6:63.

Meditation: As a child of the Most High God, there are inherent privileges available to you. With confidence and authority given by the blood of Jesus Christ, exercise these rights, and prophesy your way to victory.

Pray: Dear Lord, let the Spirit of the Word of God come alive in me as I speak that which you have placed on my heart. Healing, anointing, a heart after God, salvation, prosperity, love, purity, joy—for all this and more, I lift my voice and by faith declare these blessings over my life, the life of my family and the lives of those you have placed around me. As I speak these blessings, let them be carried on the wings of the angels of God to the throne of God. Breathe the life of God into my words, and let them come alive in the lives of us, your children. Amen.

Pray the Lord's blessing upon the cup and the bread, and then eat and drink all of it.

Day 4—Noon

Take the cup and the bread to the altar you have prepared for this sacred time.

Read 1 Corinthians 11:23–34 and 1 John 4:1–6.

Meditation: The Lord God is holy, and He desires that His children be holy, just as He is holy. You cannot handle the covenant of God deceitfully. Your intentions must be to attain to the purity and truth of Christ.

Pray: Oh Lord and Father, teach me to observe and do all that you have taught me and not to feel overwhelmed by your standard of holiness. I have the presence of the Holy Spirit to guide me, especially in times of uncertainty. Release your grace to help me appreciate the beauty of holiness. Help me to understand and apply the significance of the direction of the Holy Spirit in all my affairs. I want to find joy and fulfillment in serving you. Teach me your ways, oh Lord, that I may bring joy to your heart. I ask that I will lack nothing, but through patience become perfect and complete. Amen.

Pray the Lord's blessing upon the cup and the bread, and then eat and drink all of it.

Day 4—Evening

Take the cup and the bread to the altar you have prepared for this sacred time.

Read 1 Corinthians 2:1–16 and Philippians 4:8.

Meditation: One of the gifts presented to you at the receipt of salvation was the mind of Christ. You were given the wisdom to think like and conduct your affairs as Christ would. Manage and orchestrate your life and thoughts through the direction of the Holy Spirit.

Anointing of the Home: To anoint the door posts and lintels of your home, take a flask of pure oil, and bless it.

Pray: Holy Father, I lift up this oil to you and ask that you consecrate it to become the blood of my Lord and Savior, Jesus Christ. Amen.

Take the oil, and place it on the doors and windows of your home and property. This is symbolic of the slain Lamb of God and protection against the plagues of darkness.

Pray: Heavenly Father, I have continued in and completed these four days of fellowship and communion with you through the leading of the Holy Spirit, in meditation on your Word and in prayer. I have honored this Covenant Communion Passover and trust you by faith to build in me the character of the Lord Jesus Christ. My life is completely submitted in reverence to you, dear Lord, as I have chosen this day. Place your mark of distinction on me, because I have honored the sacrifice of Jesus Christ's blood in my life. Grant unto me the desire to completely surrender to your love and leading for the rest of my life. Amen.

Pray the Lord's blessing upon the cup and the bread, and then eat and drink all of it.

CHAPTER 16

A Peek into the Future

> Through the precious blood of Jesus Christ, I hold my future securely in my authority.

We know that the Scriptures are written for our learning. Therefore, we read them with utmost diligence so that we may apply wisdom to our decisions. What a tremendous exodus it must have been as a nation became uprooted from a lifetime of bondage. Can you envision the screams of victory and delight, the tears of joy mingled with sadness, the packing, the clamoring, the jumping for joy and the process of getting ready to leave bondage behind all rolled into over a million people? Can you hear the chatter and feel the excitement of the teenagers as they began their journey to the Promised Land? The atmosphere must have been charged with hurried delight, because the Spirit of the living God was present. They had invited His Presence in through obedience to a never-before-experienced instruction, and the fruit of their obedience was delightful.

Can you see Joshua's admiration for Moses and Aaron, and his desire to attain to the success Moses had received from God, propelling him to become Moses' servant? Can you feel Aaron's dream of becoming a priest, serving before the Lord night and day, beginning to surge again—he knew that which he envisioned was now becoming a reality. Imagine the little girls who had grown up carrying mortar beginning to giggle and play as they realized that the next day they would no longer be on the watch for the task master. Old men and women with backs bent, frail, thin and feeble from the tiring drill of stomping mortar, suddenly surging to life, energized and erect, bundling their travel package with the grin of defiance and marching to their own beat.

A new day had dawned, and each person was on the edge of what would be, each imagining life as it never had been. This God, who had executed a mighty deliverance, was going to be their God, and they would be called His people. All would be well. Provision for food, their own land, their own cities and houses of their own to dwell in with the miracle-working God watching over—this was going to be wonderful. Perhaps words cannot adequately describe the movement that led them out; it had to be felt. A mighty hand swept the people together in one accord to pack a lifetime of possessions and be out of sight by morning—the Exodus.

All went well until the first obstacle presented its dilemma. Okay, this was not any ordinary obstacle; it was the Red Sea. Visualize it with me. Take two small pebbles, the first is Egypt, and the second is the land of promise. Place them on opposite sides of a long pencil, which we will call the Red Sea. The people were trapped between Egypt and the sea. The sea is about 1,200 miles in length, so that would be impossible to go around quickly, and the width is around 190 miles, so they could not even see across to the other side. Surrounding the sea is a mountainous region, and the sound of hooves echoed, chomping furiously, ringing the bell of danger. Yes, Pharaoh had changed his mind about allowing his nation-builders to leave town, and his army was in hot pursuit.

"What, did Moses suddenly stop hearing from God? Why are we here? Did he not plan an adequate escape route? Wait, was this a trick?

Was this just false hope we got through some device or hoax Moses had used to temporarily gain Pharaoh's favor, and did Pharaoh awaken from the lull of Moses' trickery to find us gone?"

Then came the words of defeat: "We should have been left to die in Egypt; we will never survive the horror of Pharaoh's wrath. Were there not enough graves in Egypt?" Incidentally, this was not the people's first encounter with fear, and each time it reared its ugly head, it produced the same response in these children of God. Ironically, before this Exodus, while God was busy preparing to free the Israelites from the bondage of Egypt, they were busy badmouthing Moses, asking him to stop meddling in their affairs and allow them to continue being slaves. Adversity viewed through the eyes of the flesh can destroy the plans of God; viewed through the lens of faith, it is the process to the promise.

Whose shoes would you have worn in this time of chaos? Those of Moses? Those of Joshua? Those of little children with faith? Mothers with fear? Fathers who were about to be robbed once again of their freedom and stripped of their manhood and their only chance at freedom? Young girls in love who believed they could enjoy the gentleness of a husband now facing the gloom of going back to the chains of slavery and possibly death, thereby sealing their doom for love and family, or young men with the dream of being princes in the camp; leaders of teams; builders of cities; or makers of dreams who saw the distasteful enemy rising its furiously ugly head? Did Moses begin to doubt or question God? How did Moses find the answer from God to parting the Red Sea within an atmosphere charged with doubt, frustration and mad chaos?

Forget blind obedience, forget a mandated discipline, forget the rituals and rites of holy performances; once you have moved beyond the mundane and have entered the holy Presence of God, sat a while, communed with and been awed by God—once you are familiar with the path of entering into the Holy of Holies—the world and its offerings or chaos have no effect on your faith.

My mother loves the old hymn, "Steal Away, Steal Away." If God were to lead us beside the still waters all the day long (I hear a song coming), would there be any need to restore our souls? If the problems and troubles we faced were solved just the way we envisioned, would God's thoughts be higher than or equal to ours? When we tell God how to solve a problem, our ideas are humanly concocted solutions or strategies created from limited imaginations. If God worked within the framework of our imagination, would He be God?

Allow God to wow you with the wonders of heaven brought to earth, the mysteries of secret places, the treasures revealed out of darkness, and the breaking of bars of iron as He holds your hand. Allow your walk of faith to become the testimony of crooked places made straight, gates of brass broken in pieces, and doors opening and closing as you voice the will of God in spiritual warfare. Beyond it all, beyond the chaotic fervor is a timely truth to be revealed in the earth—the truth for your day that is designed to still the enemy and the avenger and answer the questions of your generation. The questions for generations past are already answered (or partially so), and as the end approaches, more truths must be revealed to parallel the advancement of evil. What if God has chosen you—your life—as the catalyst to reveal Himself through a given catastrophe? That means the circumstances and challenges will parallel the revelatory truth as well as the episodes needed to unleash that truth.

Joseph was chosen to fulfill the promise of God to Abraham, and he alone had to bear in his body the scars of fulfilling the promise. His father's love became a cherished memory as his life became wracked with the recurring theme: "Forgive! Keep your heart pure, and never lose sight of the dream." Joseph had plenty of opportunities to be bitter, lots of people to hold in unforgiveness and many dark holes in which to bury his dream.

Have you buried your dream with the shovel of unforgiveness and kept it guarded with a sour heart?

I believe that the effect of the Red Sea, the hot pursuit of Pharaoh's army and the words of doubt and bitterness stole the sweet Presence of God from the Israelites and became the beginning of the devaluing of the precious covenant they made with God at Passover. The Bible tells of the time of worship after the crossing of the Red Sea but not of the repentance of the bickering and clamoring of a people who had spouted words that had the potential to create doom.

Three days after an astoundingly monumental, divine miracle at the Red Sea, where man saw waters obey a spoken word, there was Marah. Marah represents the bitter events that present themselves, not only as mule-buck stubborn, but also with no end in sight. Again at Marah, the old pattern of solving problems trumped the power and might of their heavenly Father; yak, yak, yak, until Moses solved their problem. Two months, later the yakking started again. "Would to God we had died in Egypt." Oops—be careful what you ask for! This time, the grumbling was not for what they needed; it was for an unquenchable desire—for "bread to the full, and the flesh pots of Egypt." (Exodus 16:3)

Unbelievable the length of the rope of the sweet nothingness of sin and its ability to yank us back from progress when we begin to enter into our blessings. The noose hangs loosely around the neck and tightens ever so fiercely when it feels its ego has not been stroked—a vivid reminder that it was once in charge. Once in control indeed, but it calls the bluff, and like slaves, we melt in submission.

One after the other came gripings, and murmurings, and the eventual creation of unbelieving hearts. Could God deliver on His promise? Yes, they believed He could. However, they had developed a system of getting the hand of God to move that angered a holy God. They griped and complained. God supplied. Griped and complained. God supplied. Griped and complained, but God got tired of it.

Moses had to ask God to repent of getting tired or of being weary of His people. God judiciously came up with a solution that honored His Word and in the same breath got rid of the rebellion. Children with limited understanding would not be a part of the process, but all those who had disobeyed with knowledgeable responsibility would not enter into this promise. Then the circles began. Some died by plagues and others in war, and a great number wandered in the wilderness until they died, never entering into the land that was promised. (Numbers 14)

Was the first sign of deviation from the plan of God the sowing of the seed of rebellion? It seems as if the enemy who was determined to keep the children in bondage crept in at the first opportunity and inveigled them to break the covenant instituted through the Passover by spouting words of doom at the sight of the Red Sea, and then often enough to weary the Almighty God.

God told His children to keep the Passover yearly as a remembrance of the great deliverance from the bondage of Egypt. It seemed to have become a ritual of remembrance and not a celebration of the covenant of God by blood that was instituted to demolish yokes and strongholds. How easy it is to become suckered into the cunning of the evil one. When Jesus came, He shared the Passover as a covenant of His blood—not the traditional remembrance—and pronounced it a new covenant. The old covenant established on the blood of the Passover with the continuous shedding of the blood of animals did not have the capacity to accomplish the fulfillment of the holy law, thereby keeping God's people from rebellion and the sins that separated them from His holy Presence.

Under the terms of this new covenant, we can partake of the Passover supper—not as a ritual but for atonement. No longer do we have to live with the burns and torture of the seeds sown by the enemy, but instantly, we can be redeemed from the curse of the law through the shed blood of Jesus Christ on Calvary. In fact, we have an advocate, an intercessor, a mediator to maintain the covenant in a perpetually unbroken state. Better still, we are not limited to going to the temple, because He has built the sanctuary, the holy tabernacle, within us. Now we can come boldly to the throne of grace in times of need.

Take charge of your life and your future through the blood of Jesus Christ our Lord. Life is incomplete if all its context is based here in the natural. We must correlate the reality of the spirit by inviting God's Presence into our existence, and we know that to enter the spirit realm, we need blood. The blood chosen to enter the supernatural realm decides the results obtained and the quality of life we will live here on earth. The blood of Christ is superior to any other blood. It was shed for access to the heavenlies, but it is only available as we sit at His feet. As we humble ourselves in God's Presence, He reveals truths and strategies that counter the attacks of darkness; we see clearly through His eyes, and victory is inevitable.

CHAPTER 17

Treasures Buried in Life's Adversities

> Come unto me, all you that labor and are heavy laden, and I will give you rest. —Matthew 11:28

I revisited the story of Jacob, and as I read, I had more questions than ever. Jacob deceptively took his brother's birthright and then ran away for fear of his life. As Jacob journeyed, he found a place where he could rest for the night. I can imagine the man in deep reflection, for he now possessed the rights to his father's inheritance, yet he was on the run—a self-made fugitive from the life that had sustained him since birth and an inheritance with an attached warrant that had the license to strangle the very life out of him. This was a good time to talk with the God of his father. He took one of the stones from that place and laid it down, and as he rested he had a dream that a ladder was set on the earth, with its top reaching to heaven, and his eyes were opened— the angels of God were ascending and descending on it. When he awoke, he said, "Surely the Lord is in this place. How awesome is this place!" (Genesis 27–28)

What made it so natural for Jacob to enter into the Presence of the Lord? He built an altar, knelt upon it and entered the throne room of God as if he walked into an earthly tabernacle. We see an imperfect man who struggled with life, struggled with family, and struggled with God, deceiving and scheming his way through life even from the womb. Life did not want to be kind and yielding to Jacob, but Jacob would not accept the fate he had been dealt and was intent on defeating the secondary status expected of him. He became a man of ingenious designs, taking hold of victories through whatever means necessary, even to the point where he could be labeled a thief. However, throughout his travels, God's divine Presence and blessings never failed to work on his behalf.

What did Jacob know about God that we need to know? Failure was reversed to prosperity in the face of adversity, and he used his setbacks as valuable time to increase his profit margin. When Laban changed Jacob's wages ten times and made him work fourteen years for the woman he loved, Jacob labored willingly, seeing a great opportunity to gain more wealth than he had before, and through all this, the man continued to prosper. When it came time to reunite with his brother, whom he had defrauded of their father's inheritance, he spent one night in prayer and wrestled with a heavenly being until his request was granted. Jacob did not know how to settle for less than his heart perceived; it was not part of his nature. If you cannot see yourself defeated, you cannot be defeated, because your vision is extended onto strategies of overcoming. We see an imperfect man. He saw opportunities to destroy defeat, and defeat was not conquered temporarily, nor did he fight fire with fire; instead every obstacle was thoroughly destroyed by the power of the Most High God.

Perhaps adversity is the stepping stone to greatness. Moses was born in a time of adversity, when there was death all around, to a complaining, murmuring people who were not respected but were used to build the empire of an arrogant ruler. He rose from the rubbles of slavery to become a valuable name on the tongue of his oppressor. His mother exercised the wisdom of God, and without fear, she allowed him to grow up in the house of the enemy. The plan of God followed, because this baby became a contender for the throne of his threatened executioner. However, just before the humanistic plan played out, God divinely led Moses to the wilderness to prepare him for his God-given purpose.

You must now envision a man who was trained in royal protocol to command earthly success being transformed by the hand of the Almighty, totally saturated with humility and supernatural powers—success to the millionth degree. This was the man that went up to Mount Sinai to have a face-to-face with God. See, Moses was dissatisfied with just communing with the unknown. The yearning to see the God with whom he spoke was actually a God-given, unquenchable desire.

And God said, "I will make all my goodness pass before you, and I will proclaim the name of the Lord before you. You cannot see my face, but while my glory passes by, you shall see my back parts." (Exodus 33:19)

In order to fulfill one's call the essentials are, knowing the Name of the Lord, experiencing the goodness and grace of God; and for those who take it to the top, seeing the Lord. Do you know what Moses saw? Let's put it like this. He saw the beginning—the Spirit of God moving upon void places and commanding light, darkness, the waters, and creeping things. He saw the Word, or Christ, who was with God, as they took pleasure in creating a world they would enjoy. He saw the first surgery—Adam's rib being removed and Eve being molded from clay. He saw Noah and the rainbow and Abraham and Lot—devout men who since their first introduction never erred at being faithful to their God. He saw Joseph in Potiphar's house, resisting sin as a direct honor to his God and his values. He saw the back parts of God, what God had done before his time, the potential of God and the greatness and awesomeness of God given to us in the book of Genesis.

God needed someone to write about His works, and the desire was placed in Moses' heart to see God. This revelatory vision then transformed his potential to lead from a mere earthly perspective to the vision and revelation needed to become the greatest leader to grace the earth, and thereby fulfill his purpose.

When we see God, the rest is history. When we envision the potential of God, we are unlimited. We capture the span of our lives with past, present, and future obstacles; we bottle them and remove them from the realm of probability into the realm of great accomplishments, then enjoy life to its fullest. When we grasp the revelation of God and how to enter into His presence, we do not lament at the adversity around us. Instead, we continue to prosper by moving in a realm of glory that supersedes the physical. We can even enter the dwellings of the executioner and thrive.

Jesus said, "The hand of the betrayer is with me on the table, the table of the Lord." (Luke 22:21) Jesus was not perturbed by Judas and the betrayal that was brewing. In fact, He let none of the twelve, His closest, know a betrayer was in their midst. Jesus was not even perturbed by the crucifixion, for He went willingly to the cross, choosing His Father's will over His fleshly desires. These men knew that buried in the adversities of life were treasures that would leave true, untainted legacies that would ultimately propel the earth to its culmination. Not legacies that would last a generation or two, but legacies that melded heaven and earth together and furthered the heart of God.

Jacob was blessedly taught by Isaac and Rebecca to enter into the Holy of Holies as if it were an earthly tabernacle. He was not limited by thought, tradition, or even his sin. However, before he embarked on the warpath to take his life back, he looked for an opportunity to be in great favor with God. His brother, Esau, had been handed the firstborn legacy of carrying on the family's inheritance, which included not only the increase of the physical estate, but also the covenant of God that a nation would be born of his loins. Jacob knew that he who had the covenant had undeniable access and favor with Almighty God. I do not believe that the exchange of the red stew was an isolated incident; it was an opportunity that was long sought and impeccably timed. Sure his brother would regret it, but Jacob saw this treasure as worth the trouble. Upon possession of this covenant, the unlimited abundance and audience with God was his forever.

Jacob walked into God's Presence with boldness, knowing that he was now the heir of the promise God gave his father, Abraham. In his physical body was the promise of a holy God, and God would not deny him access. He learned to enter in and communicate with God as he exercised his rights to this great treasure. In the times he needed council or comfort, or through the time he had to serve additionally for the bride he loved, Jacob could have chosen various modes of action or reaction. Instead, we see the unfolding of a unique strategy that made him great in the earth. His success was inherited through entering into the Presence of God, and blood was the offering he gave for this great privilege.

Can we conceive this phenomenon? Are we ready to make this eternal covenant with the Almighty God? Can we cast off the spell of blindness? Can we enter in with confidence and the blood of Jesus Christ, our Savior? It is clear that greatness in the earth is born of those who communicate in the spiritual realm. Let's up the ante. Lasting spiritual success is for those who communicate with the true and living God.

You know when the promise is in your physical temple. You know when you have the unique gift, talent or offering for which the earth is waiting. You know when the hope of Christ for the world has been deposited in you. To sell out to the realms of darkness just to hasten or fulfill God's gift inside is just plain foolish. To tap into God through Christ is not as glaringly open as we would like it, but the passion of the gift will drive us to cry out at God's feet until He empowers us with the key to open up the treasure inside without the gut-wrenching guilt and death that comes with a sellout. The Spirit of the Lord awaits our coming to usher us into the Lord's Presence. The Word is nigh us, even in our mouths. Let's take our eyes, ears, and hearts and rip them away from the bitterness of the glitter of the earth. Saints, the glory is not found on the earth; it is hidden with the Lord.

CHAPTER 18

Authority in the Blood

Behold, I come quickly: hold fast that which you have, that no man take your crown. —Revelation 3:11

As we reflect on the choices of life here in the earth, we see man acquiring, conquering, building, and enjoying the earth. However, involvement and choices on a spiritual plane take a bit more than ingenious imagination. There are no real requirements or hard-and-fast rules laid down for man to follow regarding this plane, and with *free will,* one has to make choices based on understanding. But as we look at religion, we knit our brows and ask the question—not only with our bodies, but also with our hearts—"Is there really more?" Unless provoked, it feels better to ignore the gory details of the unknown, but the trouble is that the unknown is intriguingly provocative.

Far beyond provocation, across the spectrum of desire, man has searched out religious involvement to empower him to activate earthly success, and this could be as simple as asking for healing. I say *religion,* because religion is really the seeking of help beyond human ability, which requires dedicated commitment to serving the hand implored or simply worshiping that which empowers us and bestows the earthly and spiritual gifts we seek. Absolutely, at its core, religion requires worship—or in more adequate terms, it requires devotion—and those who partake relinquish their choice when it comes to worship. Hence, as man gives himself over to the worshiping of his chosen god, especially the gods or the God of the spirit realm, he is handed a measure of authority to command supernatural activity on the earth.

The point is that the spiritual realm is dead without man's involvement. A simple way to state this is that you cannot have a party without friends. Prepare the goodies, plan the activities and take out the gadgets, but without someone to share these things, you are all alone. It is no wonder God went through the agony of sending His Son, the Lord Jesus Christ, to redeem mankind, for God desires our friendship. He has so much love to give. He prepared the toys, created man, then regularly came to enjoy the sweet fellowship His heart desired. After man was tricked into disobedience, God did not give up but persisted in creating an avenue of escape. I can imagine how glorious it is for those who have chosen to enter His courts and fellowship with Him—how much He must lavish His wonderful, amazing riches and abundant love and knowledge on them. As His own gain knowledge of this intriguing world and begin to navigate it, we see the amazing effects and wonderful changes in the lives all around.

Let's go back to the matter of blood. Man is granted authority to wield the efficacy of blood upon the earth (whether blood used for evil or the blood of Jesus Christ). This is a great time to say that the use of any blood for spiritual activity other than the blood of Jesus Christ, is evil. As a result, you are not innocent, oh man, but held totally accountable—whoever you are and with whomever or whatever you have conspired to do with blood. Have you pled the blood of Jesus Christ over your family for generations to come? Then know that with efficacy and authority, your request has been granted spiritually, and you have placed full responsibility on yourself for the outcome of these generations, as you have required blood of the Spirit upon them.

Blood is the spiritual tool available on the earth for the purpose of prying open the treasures of the heavenly realm—treasures big and small, dark and ugly, wonderful and glorious. As blood is shed in the earth to access these treasures, be absolutely sure that a spirit or the Spirit will answer. Think of blood as currency, and the treasures as objects that are available on sale in that realm. Have you ever attempted to purchase an item with the correct monetary equivalence and been denied the purchase? Vendors are eager to part with their wares just like the gifts and treasures of the spirit, where there exists an unlimited warehouse waiting to be tapped into. The goodies, gadgets, and activities are all on sale, waiting to be purchased by those who find them useful.

Lucifer's dark and foreboding curses and spells and all those demonic activities only require blood. I truly don't believe they even require faithfulness, because nothing pure, sacred or good is in his nature; but surely the gifts imparted carry within them the painful horror of the darkness and death intrinsic to that kingdom. No matter how glazed the demonic gifts are with the thrill and dazzle of glamour, at the heart of those gifts reign death—inescapable death. However, they do require worship. That swindler wants glory. Oh, yes! Perhaps the only thing that keeps evil happy is that you show out, show off, and parade your dark treasure for all to see.

"The Blood Will Never Lose Its Power" is a song penned by a famous writer, and it is amazingly true. Jesus' blood is always available to the saints, the children of the Most High God. Nope, it is not available to those who have not been born again. Just the legalities of the Kingdom of God— not an offense, and its wonder-working resurrecting power has not diminished one iota. The sweetest, most tantalizing clause in this matter is that the blood of Jesus Christ our Lord silences the blood spilled for demonic activity. Through Christ's new covenant, His blood is accessed through intercession, supplication and all kinds of prayer. We must simply ask God in faith. Through taking bread and wine or fruit juice in a covenant, blessing it in the name of the Lord Jesus Christ and then partaking by eating—similar to the Passover.

Approximately fifty days after the ascension of our Lord Jesus Christ, a supernatural outpouring came to earth to dwell in the form of God's Holy Spirit. There was a party in the upper room in Jerusalem where Jesus' disciples were gathered, praying and waiting for the dispatch from heaven that would accompany them and teach them how to acquire greater and greater accomplishments on the earth. As each person tasted of this magnificent infilling of the Spirit, a portion of the life of God was deposited in them that manifested in bringing salvation, encouragement, and a greater glory that continues today.

Saul of Tarsus became converted to the gospel of the Lord Jesus Christ and spoke of his visit to the heavenly realm, saying he saw things that were unlawful to utter on the earth. In many of his writings, he admonished the Church of the living God to walk in the authority that God had given to them. By believing in Jesus Christ and His shed blood, the Church is empowered to triumph over evil. "For we wrestle not against flesh and blood." (Ephesians 6:12). A note worthy of mention is that the Scripture refers to obstacles in the earthly realm using the term *blood,* yet it indicates that to overcome, our fight takes place in the heavenly realm against rankings of demonic powers.

Consider men who resist the will of God and commit sin; why didn't the Bible say they fight against God? Because by submitting to evil, men serve sin and become slaves to its demand, creating wealth for its master and staging a sort of indirect competition against the increase of the kingdom of God. To serve the enemy is to destroy the precious lives of brothers and sisters, carving out subtle and devious crafts that break their spirits. The continuous breaking and wrestling weakens those lives to bring surrender to darkness. We can agree that sin is disobedience to God, but God is not duped or overthrown by our disobedience. Sin can be categorized as a stench or stupor that we conjure, and as the violator indulges, the stench creates a suffocating mist over the lives we share; they, too, become broken and weakened by its effect. No wonder the Bible tells us that leaders will have the greater punishment, because leaders command a powerful sway over those who follow. To yield to the cunning craftiness of sin as a leader is to destroy those whom we serve.

God told King Saul of Israel that rebellion against God is as the sin of witchcraft, and stubbornness is as iniquity and idolatry. God then rejected this man as a leader of His people, because through his disobedience to the Word of God and a stubborn heart that wanted its own righteousness, he produced witchcraft and allowed God's people to sink into sin. Saul rejected God's way and the purity of God's Word, substituting it for that which appeased his followers, and God rejected him as a leader. Every leader is under authority and given great insight into the strategies and designs to build the empire entrusted to him or her. We must be vigilant so that the roaring lion whose sole business is to devour our calling comes nowhere close to our hearts or to our flock with the cunning wiles that overthrow greatness. Let's labor with God against the gates of hell and receive the crown of life prepared for those who overcome.

In all of this, I believe that triumphing over darkness, even as we see it manifesting itself through people, is the initial protocol of faith. After managing, confusing, binding, and subduing evil in the earth, the real authority is to take of the gadgets of the Spirit and show to the earth the manifest glory and power of our risen Savior. John says, "There is no greater love than when a man lays down his life for his friend." The laying down of Jesus' life not only ensured godly access to the spirit realm, but also settled us in Christ so that we may blaze the trail of righteousness through love so that our loved ones and others may follow. This is not a command, requirement or hard-and-fast rule. We simply touch the heart of God and pull our hands away only to find the pulse of God coursing through our veins with authority and the sanctity of love. Then, with contagious zeal, we grab someone else, and then someone else, and beckon them to come and experience the awesome mystery.

The covenant of promise, then, is not only for a chosen few but for the whomsoever will, to bring about the pulse of God in the earth. As we enter the heavenlies by the Spirit of the living God, we see our names along with our assignments, and we become unstoppable as we run to gain the prize of the high calling in Christ Jesus our Lord.

CHAPTER 19

The Destroyer

How shall we escape if we neglect such great salvation?
—Hebrews 2:3

In every entity, hierarchy is structured to govern, manage, and ensure success. The same is true of the spirit realm. Authoritarian ranks are established with specific assignments, specific powers, and for specific locations.

In the domain of hell, we learn the names of hierarchical spirits through the book of Ephesians—namely, principalities, powers, might, dominion and spiritual wickedness in high places. Principalities are first in place, time and rank. These are rulers at the introduction of a concept or of an individual's life even by a spoken word. Powers are spirits that have taken control of and influence or have become masters of human lives, because they have been granted the authority to do so. Might are the spirits able to work miraculous signs on the earth. Dominion denotes power and lordship of how one's life is governed—control. Spiritual wickedness represents wicked and malicious plots of iniquity and inconceivable evil that stuns the earth and sends mankind into shock upon its manifestation.

In the book of Daniel, the account is given of an angel of God informing Daniel that his prayers had been answered from the first day he began his intercession. However, the Prince of Persia withstood the answer from the heavenly realms. The account goes on to state that reinforcement was sent to the angel as Michael, one of the chief princes of God's angel, helped him to overcome the battle against the demonic Persian prince and bring the answers to Daniel (Daniel 10).

We can well imagine that battles are fought and won in the spirit realm daily. Angels increase in strength through the prayers of the saints as the will of God is voiced and Jehovah God supplies victory for His kingdom. Saints of the Most High God are given the authority on earth to command the activities of the spirit realm. Prayer and intercession are wielded as the Sword of the Spirit or the Word of God. God then watches over His Words to perform it.

At what time did Daniel have angelic visitations? At the time of the evening or daily sacrifice, in times of prayer. At what time did Peter and John perform the miracle of healing the lame man in the book of Acts? At the hour of prayer. Though Hannah mourned for years about her barrenness, when did God choose to answer her cry? The day she went to the temple to pray. Indulge me still. As Jesus prepared for His crucifixion He went away on a mountain to pray. The book of Luke records that "as He prayed" He was transfigured from natural to supernatural and conversed with Moses and Elijah, who, in the realms of the heavenlies are with God. Prayer is the vehicle that ushers us into the presence of the Almighty God. Have we forfeited our miracles by not praying? Was it this time of prayer that caused Jesus not to fail during His greatest trial?

If there is a perfect means to state the importance of continuous prayer, it should be proclaimed. It is absolutely imperative that the saints pray without ceasing. Imagine a war taking place in the heavenlies for the life of a teenager we will call Timothy. Timothy lives in Rocky Point. The spirit of death was given the assignment to manifest itself in Timothy through the form of suicide, hatred, or a freak accident—so death has been lurking around Timothy and stirring up trouble to bring about its plans.

The saints living in Rocky Point have the jurisdictional authority to bind the spirit of death that has come for Timothy. The Holy Spirit will reveal this heavenly information to the heart of the child's mother or any other family member or close friend, and most importantly, to an intercessor or prophet. If the information revealed is brought to the throne of God through the petition of prayer and the binding of the foul spirit of death, the angels of God are strengthened and able to defeat the spirits of darkness. (Note carefully that Jesus told us how to handle spirits of evil. We can bind them, cast them out or command them to leave. We should be mindful that our prayers must follow Christ's teachings).

Let's say the revelation was ignored—perhaps because of ignorance or even because no one cared to stand in the gap for the youngster. Another strategy would have to be employed in the spirit. The Lord could draw on a prayer ushered years ago over Timothy's life or reveal this knowledge to intercessors or prophets elsewhere in the world. Our advocate in heaven, Jesus Christ, could also petition for his life to be spared. Finally, it could be that the presence of the Lord could be felt by Timothy himself, and Timothy could speak the will of God in the situation and be saved from the attack.

John got a glimpse of the glory of the Lord Jesus Christ in Revelation 1.

I was in the Spirit on the Lord's day, and heard behind me a great voice, as of a trumpet, "Saying, I am Alpha and Omega, the first and the last" ... and out of His mouth went a sharp two edged sword: and His countenance was as the sun shines in his strength. And when I saw Him, I fell at His feet as dead. And He laid His right hand upon me, saying unto me, "Fear not; I am the first and the last: I am He that lives, and was dead; and, behold, I am alive for evermore, Amen; and have the keys of hell and of death." (Revelation 1:10-18)

Then in Ephesians 1, we learn that all this authority from He who is alive forevermore, along with the spirit of wisdom and revelation in the knowledge of Christ, was given to the Church by Christ Jesus Himself. Why? Because by obedience in fulfilling the will of His Father, Christ obtained the glory of the Name that is above all names, had all things placed under His feet and is now the head over all things to command as He so desires. The Church, which is Christ's body, extends in the earth as His arms, legs, heart, head; you get the picture. Obedience to God sure yields a ton of wonder.

Death, therefore, is held captive by those who are in Christ Jesus and who possess the revelatory knowledge to prevent its untimely demise. Yes, the Bible says the last enemy that will be defeated is death, and then Christ will subject Himself to the Father God so that God may be all in all (1 Corinthians 15). This means the saints will go the way of death but not with the sting of death. This is part of the inheritance for the saints who are not beguiled by that which empowers death—that is, not beguiled by sin. The saints who live their lives in the will of God are rendered free from untimely deaths.

Jesus told His disciples many times that His time of death had not yet come, and when it came, He humbly embraced the path in order to accomplish the heart of His Father. Death did not conquer Christ; instead, He submitted to the process in order to enter the realms and domain of death and strip its authority over those who abandon themselves to His care.

Now all other spirits of hell are subject to Christ. Sickness and disease—even though they seem so formidable and uncontrollable—have been rendered powerless to the Name and blood of the Lord Jesus Christ. The spirits of lust, greed, murder, pride and poverty, and all the other dark spirits of hell, have been made subject to Him. Colossians 1:16 says, "For by him were all things created, that are in heaven, and that are in earth, visible and invisible, whether they be thrones, or dominions, or principalities, or powers: all things were created by him, and for him."

Through the power of His resurrection, Christ has placed all things under His feet. Then He made known to His Bride, the Church (now called the body of Christ), the mystery of His will, and since this is His body, there is an exceeding greatness of power that works for the Church. This power only works in union with Christ's established mode of how He has set forth His power to work. This heavenly power cannot be manipulated or used in the context of man's desire and design—only according to the protocol Christ has set up by His authority to defeat and subdue the realms of darkness.

The advantage to serving the Lord our God with all our hearts, souls and minds is crystal clear. The first order of truth is that there is absolutely no uncertainty regarding life or death when a follower of Christ has surrendered his or her life to the care of the Lord. In matters of life, the Holy Spirit teaches and guides us in the principles of Christ. To follow these principles wholeheartedly is to gain the spiritual knowledge necessary for success in every area of our lives here on earth. In death, it becomes "absent from the body, present with the Lord." (2 Corinthians 5:8)

In the case of little Timothy and the war that hell has chosen to wage over his life, the mother may say, "I did not hear God. In fact, I have never heard God speak." However, listen carefully to the stories of the events surrounding the time of this unusual incident and the signs are clear. Sometimes the signs are reversed; little Timothy became extremely disobedient and defiant prior to the incident. The sign could be the introduction of a new friend whose behavior was blatantly contradictory to the family's values and set off warning bells. Another bell could toll in the mind of a parent figure, urging that person to spend time with Timothy or get closer to him. One thing is sure; God never leaves Himself without a witness, and even though we discount our place with God with labels of, '*I am unworthy*,' '*Why would God speak to me*?' '*I'm not a Christian*,' '*I do not even believe in God*,' these statements do not change God's faithfulness to do for His children what a genuinely loving Father would do.

God is not a man and does not conduct His lordship on the levels of mankind's ideology. Rejection does not lock God into a mode of sorrow and dismay. When people choose another god, this does not ruffle His feathers. Botched ideas of who God is or twisted modes of giving Him service cannot subject Him to change. God is unchangeable. In fact, God is governed by His Word, and His Word is already established. We can probably say that God is on autopilot, cruising to the end—the end of time as we know it. But that would not be a fair analogy. I believe our heavenly Father—the Almighty God of Abraham, Isaac and Jacob; the great I AM—is busy orchestrating the notes of our lives so that we may come to know Him. Think of a newborn baby and the love and care of the mother and father. Soon the baby recognizes that there is only one Ma and only one Pa; then as time glides by, there is no doubt who that child will identify as parents. God is working to gain our trust.

When the Lord God instituted the Passover, He told His children of its purpose. He said, "The blood will be a sign for you wherever you are, and when I see the blood, the destroyer will pass over you." (Exodus 12:13). For me, the best part of the purpose of the blood of Christ is that the destroyer cannot come in with its plagues to destroy those under its care.

Fast-forward to the end of the book, where John, the revelator on the Isle of Patmos, caught visions of heaven and earth at the time of the end. In chapter 15 of his revelation, he described a scene in heaven where the Tabernacle of Testimony was opened and angels of God with plagues came out of the temple to place destruction on the earth. In Exodus 25, God told Moses to place the God-given testimony in the Ark of the Covenant, below the mercy seat, and God would meet with him there. In Revelation 12, John saw Satan and his demons cast out of heaven, and a voice spoke saying the saints would overcome the Devil that had been cast out, by the blood of the Lamb of God and the word of their testimony—that is, the dedicated saints who loved not their lives unto death. In Chapter 19, the angel continued his explanation of the mysteries John encountered. John was in awe and wanted to worship the angel, but the angel told him to worship God, for they both were recipients of the testimony of Jesus, which is the Spirit of prophecy. As the heavens opened, John saw Him who is called, *Faithful and True* and *The Word of God*, clothed with a robe dipped in blood, on which He had the name written, "KING OF KINGS AND LORD OF LORDS."

Piece this puzzle together. Obedience and worship of Almighty God pave the way for us to enter the spiritual realm by the blood of Jesus. As the saints submit to Christ, not having their own righteousness, they are enlightened to faithfully overcome the Devil, thereby producing a testimony acceptable to God, that which can be placed in the covenant of His presence. All together, this generates the Spirit of prophecy, which is also the Word—Christ, spoken by the saints prophetically and honored by God Himself, which becomes the authority that overcomes the plagues, the destroyer that wastes the life of man.

CHAPTER 20

The Business of Christ's Redemption

For if the trumpet gives an uncertain sound who shall prepare himself for the battle? —1 Corinthians 14:8

It is abundantly clear that life does not only originate and terminate on earth, but there is a continuation to it all. There is much more to being alive than the physical eye can perceive or the limited mind can process. Navigation through the unknown produces its own challenges (as if those of our lives are not enough). Pausing to face uncertainty can take the wind out of our sails, especially if the guide of this most important task has never experienced the journey. One thing is certain, no one wants to be dead wrong.

The Spirit of promise, by which we are sealed in Christ through the Holy Spirit when we trust in the preached Word of the gospel of salvation, weeds out the webs of uncertainty and bestows on us an inheritance as we become the possession of Christ, purchased by His redeeming blood. Hold it! This wonderful promise is only effective when we become the glory of Christ. Sealed in Christ, yes; trust in the preached Word, yes; purchased by redemption, yes; possessors of the riches of Christ's inheritance, yes; knowledgeably walking away from the precepts laid down by the Spirit of promise, no. Redemption by Christ's blood and its benefits leads us into victory with Christ; that is how we become sealed—through redemptive victory, not redemptive failures.

We cannot keep riding the donkey of failure at the task God handed to us to produce glory for His kingdom; it is going round in circles. The process and the end are exclusively for God's glory, not ours—and this glory is not the fading glory that comes with excuses of failure. We would like to think that omission of one still ratifies the others. However, the same power that ensures the one, ensures all. Joshua fought the battle at Jericho and the walls crumbled. Gideon won his battle with a third of his army; or, we could say, one-third of his potential. The three Hebrew boys stood their ground only to be thrown into the fiery furnace, but walked out of the furnace alive as a testimony to the infinite glory and lengths God will go to defend His chosen. However, when we return from our God-given assignments—sometimes with the stamp of the enemy's defeat branded on our foreheads, and our Christian walk all muddled and distorted, we explain why God allowed the defeat.

Please, we cannot fool ourselves into thinking we can somehow negotiate the terms of this promise; really, it is not even negotiable by God Himself. His Word is already given. For God to breach His Word is equivalent to Him relinquishing His throne. Not going to happen—not now, not ever. But why would we excuse failure? It does not glorify the power of God; it merely sheds reproach on God's kingdom. How about excelling beyond the set goal? Now that is an exciting proposition. If we trust in the Spirit of promise, let's exceed the boundaries in a blaze of glory.

Dredge the past so it won't block your future. When we began the journey, wholeheartedly believing in the promise, we stood spiritually to take the helm of righteousness and declared that we were counted with those who have washed their robes in white. As soon as we took the stand, the monster of defeat and shame rose up from the scum of past sins. Quickly and shamefully we submitted to its ruse and cowered in fear, thinking it had the authority to defeat us and scar our lives.

Let's flip the script. The past and its ugliness create a mess for those outside of the protection and blood of Jesus Christ—those who are not part of His body. When I am the hand of the Lord Jesus Christ, I am stretched forth in love and tenderness to bring help and healing to the earth. Is Christ defeated? Is Christ ashamed? Is Christ intimidated by my past sins? Of course not! Rise up from the crippling effects of failure through the blood of the Lord Jesus Christ. The promise was not given in ignorance; it abounds with wisdom and spiritual insight to slice completely the head of the spirits of darkness that wish to trouble us.

Weakness of the flesh is subject to healing through the plan of salvation. Don't give in on account of the whisperings of darkness. Hold your head high in the power of your resurrected Lord, not in your past sins or future accomplishments; neither of these belong to us. Past sins belong to the Devil. Let him keep them. Let him nourish and keep them alive, for they were enforced on us by trickery—but really, they belong to him. Let him have those sins. Success and glory belong to our Father God; success was bought and paid for with the precious blood of our Lord and Savior, Jesus Christ. In fact, the more we honor the Lord God with our achievements, the more He bestows on us. This is called a sorting of priorities.

Did Christ submit to the offers of sin so His kingdom could advance? That is equal to raising a banner over our ministry titled "Dumb Betrayal". Proceed in Christ with all wisdom and understanding, presenting your body as a living, breathing, sacrificial offering, buffeted and tossed while you enjoy the ride in Christ. Know that this earthly tabernacle is the signature of Christ in the earth, and it must write His truth, love, and grace on every heart it touches. Christ is called the Word when He is spoken on the earth, and Christ is manifested on the earth at the written

Word of God. I must speak and write that the earth be filled with the beauty of the Lord.

Every living adult can testify that at some point in life, he or she came into the experience of *God*—undeniable God, the Word manifested. The difficulty was in sustaining the experience. It seemed very real and tangible but elusive and past-finding. Trying to tap into that experience again was like using a straw to navigate the ocean. Even more disappointing was that many of those who claimed to know God did not lead well enough that a path could be followed. As a result, we try to regain the experience through other means. But God is not for the superstitious, not available to the thrill seeker, will not prove Himself upon demand (as He has nothing to prove or lose), is not on display so money can command His auspices, does not bow to kings and lords, is not summoned by supernatural powers, and certainly is not found by the dead.

How is God found, and by whom? Where is He, that I may enter His courts? How can I distinguish Him from that which is not God?

God is found by the diligent seekers who seek Him with all our hearts. What can a man give in exchange for his soul? The soul sometimes erects barriers of pride and earthly desires and even impatience that divert and rob the true meaning of man's existence we call life. Even though God's expression is everywhere, we must get beyond the expressions and find His heart. Do not be deceived; whatever a man sows, he will reap. Sow to the diligence of self-denial of earthly attractions that beckon like neon signs in the dark of night, and reap the eternal reward of hearing God's heartbeat.

You will know you have found God when He sits on the throne of your heart. You will know His Son, the Lord Jesus Christ, when you have left all to follow Him. Repentance marks the starting point, and faith fuels the velocity of the find. You will find the joy of His Presence when He becomes your Lord of all.

Why should I depend on God? His thoughts are far wiser than mine, His plans are certainly greater, and His vision more perfect for the path ahead.

God does not leave Himself without a witness. He is not a man and does not communicate on levels sold out to the intellect. We ought not to think that God is like gold, silver, or stone, graven by art and man's device. Would an inventor abandon his successful invention? Would an artist discard her best painting? Would God deny you audience when He holds the certificate to your existence? He communicates to a pure heart. He is not far from us, as we are His offspring. Therefore, we must scale the hurdles that divide and reach for the assurance of God with us that is guaranteed by the hope of glory.

In Hebrews chapter 9 the writer paints a picture of two spiritual positions available to us. First is the worldly sanctuary where the candlestick, table, and showbread were found. Interpreted, outward decorations with functional qualities necessary for worship, but made by man. All we need is man-centered efforts to keeps us in this outer court. Then came the second veil, or the Holiest of All, with the golden sensor, ark of the covenant, the golden pot of Manna, Aaron's rod that budded, and the tablet of the covenant. The High Priest alone entered into the Holiest where the miraculous power of God was displayed, and he could not enter this holy place without blood. The shadow and copy of the old covenant has passed; now we enter the holiest with the blood of Christ that washes and purifies even our very conscience from dead works. Until the purification from dead works is manifested in us, we will continue the drama of the branding of the works of sin with consciences oblivious to righteousness. To celebrate carnality is a testimony of living in the outer court, and this is easy because the outer court is still viewed as the temple.

"Let no man deceive you by any means." (2 Thessalonians 2:3) The redemption of Christ works to enlighten us against the working of Satan who comes with the power and signs of lying wonders. Satan works only with lies. Once we believe that lie, we then become the lie.

Once we become the lie, the spirit that works in us controls us and we can no longer detect a lie. If we cannot detect a lie, then how can we know the truth? (You shall know the truth and the truth shall set you free—St. John 8:32) How can I know what is true?

And then shall that Wicked be revealed, whom the Lord shall consume with the spirit of His mouth, an shall destroy with the brightness of His coming: Even him, whose coming is after the working of Satan with all power and signs and lying wonders, and with all deceivableness of unrighteousness in them that perish; because they received not the love of the truth, that they might be saved. And for this cause God shall send them strong delusion, that they should believe a lie: That they all might be damned who believed not the truth, but had pleasure in unrighteousness. (2 Thessalonians 2:8-12)

The business of redemption, or the "paid in full" guarantor, can only be accessed by truth and faith. Redemption is not just a performance of rituals and commandments. Redemption is a calling that is heeded by the strong and the daring, for it takes supernatural abilities to escape the grip and bondage of hell. Can my heart hear and acknowledge truth, and run after it until I find and harness it? Can I keep the focus necessary and not lose sight amidst the blinding glare of half-truths? What are my priorities, where are my spiritual investments? Satisfaction of the senses increases in strength with each surrender. Therefore, my dictates must be plucked from the temperament of my senses and yielded to the holiness and love of God. Redemption is gained as I yield my intellect and all reinforced chains of limited reasoning to the sovereign will of the Almighty God.

CHAPTER 21

Then Comes the End

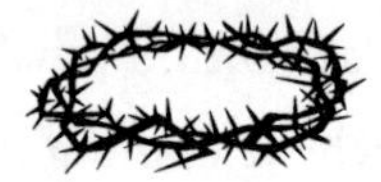

> He that overcomes shall inherit all things; and I will be his God, and he shall be my son. —Revelation 21:7

This breathtaking opportunity for the discovery of life that continues to amaze us must not control and subdue our intellects. Instead, life must be lived at the pace and standards we set from hearts dedicated to serving the Almighty God. Think of the array of knowledge available today compared to days of old, and you can appreciate that time and seeking are the masters of knowledge. Then the question to be answered is this: Who masters our time so that the seeking may become rewarding? My husband teaches, "Time cannot be regained or recaptured, use it wisely."

You will agree with me that only few have cheated death—and some only temporarily. Time governs our lifespan, and negotiations for extensions are futile. When death requires a response, it must be supplied. Are you ready to go? Are you ready to say goodbye to it all? Have you prepared for the afterlife? Surely, after the end comes the beginning—of what?

What will *you* say in the face of death? It will pose that question and require an answer to the new beginning. Certainly wisdom dictates that the question be answered now rather than then, for death is sure. No need to complicate the matter, just a simple answer will do.

Remember in class, on an exam paper, one must answer *true* or *false; a, b, c,* or *d;* or simply pencil in a response. Mastering knowledge did give us something to say. Then came the teacher, and we waited with bated breath to hear the truth. Remember how sure you were that a given answer was correct, only to find it wrong? Goodness, it sparked a fire inside—a sense that the error could have been avoided with a little more diligence, especially because it lowered the score. "You know, I was going for the *A*. Next time." Unfortunately, with death, there is no *next time*—not even after playing the cards and experiencing fortune at our hands in this life. Death is real and sorely demanding.

If the trend is true, the search may contain the answer. The quest for knowledge has solved trillions of matters. Here are two little gems from Proverbs. "The spirit of man is the candle of the Lord." (Proverbs 20:27) "Through desire a man, having separated himself, seeks and intermeddles with all wisdom." (Proverbs 18:1) The difference between the searching-out of life and the search for life is that the untiring, ruthless darts of evil that are portrayed as satisfying must not have dominion over the soul. All the alluring solutions that can propel my status in this life cannot outweigh the prominence and value of my soul and its priority at any given moment of life. For as sure as flies follow dead ointments putrefied from the filth of decay, so demons follow the offerings of sin, and ignorance of God's law is no excuse. What a joke to try and pull the innocence card in the face of death.

Until I discover whose I am, I will always be the servant of the one who has discovered and mastered the game of life, live in the shadow of the clever or be ruled by standards set for me by another. I must know and set in course my design and destiny in order to rise above the throng. The kicker is that the search is beyond my capacity of reasoning. That which I can see, touch, taste, and handle has already, in some dimension, been conquered and does not contain sustainable or abundant life, for given time, these things pass on. So that which my soul cries for is the truth of the uncharted path of victory—a tale that can expressly be told by the dead.

Let's gather stories of the claims of death, for perhaps there lays the answer. No, no, for the margin of error is beyond statistical acceptance. Let's try to navigate death by chance and see if we can conjure any similar experiences. No, no, the uncertainty is too uncertain. Let's wait until the end; it cannot be all that bad. Well, here again, sanity dictates that this reasoning has too many holes. It feels like this mystery could drive one mad just searching for truth.

In the hour of His greatest trial, as He hung on the cross for the sins of mankind, Jesus cried out to His father, "Do not forsake me, oh God." At the end, as we transverse the planes of life in search for that which will never die, be certain that the weight of choice will bear upon our hearts like a millstone hurled into the sea. Then from our inner being we will sound the cry for mercy from him whom we have served, with full knowledge that the end has come and dominion has shifted from man to God. Alone in that hour as we make our final pleas and close this chapter of life, let the eternal God and Jesus Christ His son be the name that echoes through our eternity.

Okay, if you believe with all your heart that your life is truly important, say with me, "Dear Lord Jesus, son of the living God and Christ of this world, please come and live in my heart. I truly repent of my rebellious and evil ways that are contrary to your truth, and I invite you to be Lord of my life and to sit on the throne of my heart. I renounce and turn away from my past and its darkness. Please Lord, give me assurance of your Presence and teach me how to dedicate the rest of my life to you. By faith I believe you have forgiven me of my sins and violations of your Word.

I claim the born-again experience and will partake of water by baptism and the blood of the promise given to the Saints. I dedicate the rest of my life to finding, worshiping and fulfilling your will for my life. I am yours, Father God, through Christ Jesus, now and forevermore. Amen."

CPSIA information can be obtained
at www.ICGtesting.com
Printed in the USA
FSOW02n1625100717
36139FS